NA'EDA
OUR FRIENDS

By Alexandra J. McClanahan
and
Hallie L. Bissett

Foreword by Susan A. Anderson

Edited by Veldee Hall

The CIRI Foundation is the recipient of any proceeds
from the sale of this book.

The CIRI Foundation
Anchorage, Alaska

Also by The CIRI Foundation:

Alaska Scrapbook: Moments in Alaska History

A Place for Winter, Paul Tiulana's Story

A Reference in Time, Alaska Native History Day by Day

Growing Up Native in Alaska

Our Stories, Our Lives

Putting Up Fish On The Kenai

Reflections on the Alaska Native Experience

Sakuuktugut

Cover Photography: ©1996 Chris Arend

Cover Design: Amanda L. Rothbarth

Graphic Design: Hal Gage, Gage Photo Graphics, Anchorage, Alaska

Na'eda means "our friends" in Dena'ina Athabascan. The CIRI Foundation is grateful to Eklutna Elder Alberta Stephan and Professor Alan Boraas for their assistance in naming the book. Stephan is familiar with the Upper Cook Inlet Dena'ina and Copper River Athabascan dialects. As a small child in the 1920s, Stephan lived near her grandmother Olga Nikolai Ezi, who was the wife of Chief Simeon Ezi. Stephan's father, Pete Ezi, was her grandparents' second son. Stephan credits her grandmother for teaching her much about her Athabascan culture. Stephan is the author of *The First Athabascans of Alaska: Strawberries*, and *Cheda (Athabascan Indian for grandma)*. Boraas teaches anthropology at Kenai Peninsula College, a branch of the University of Alaska Anchorage. He has taught a Dena'ina language and mythology class since 1988, first with Peter Kalifornsky and later with Donita Peter from Tyonek. Together with James Kari, he edited *A Dena'ina Legacy K'tl'egh'i Sukdu, The Collected Writings of Peter Kalifornsky*.

The cover photo was made along Turnagain Arm near Falls Creek. The Native artwork from throughout Alaska is courtesy of the Alaska Native Medical Center Auxiliary Gift Shop.

Foreword

Alaska Native corporations and tribal organizations, addresses and maps are included in our expanded and revised *Na'eda, Our Friends*, in what we hope is a convenient and handy reference. Our goal is to combine maps, a basic primer on Native issues surrounding ANCSA, and a directory in an easily transportable book.

This volume lists addresses and phone numbers for the 13 Native regional corporations, 173 village corporations (including the 4 urban corporations for Kenai, Sitka, Ketchikan and Juneau), 231 traditional/IRA councils, six former reserves and Alaska's only reservation, Metlakatla. Also listed are major non-profits, members of the Alaska Native Education Consortium, other important educational organizations, and culture centers and museums.

In this new edition of *Na'eda*, we have added web sites and emails for all of the listings for which these can be obtained. In addition to listing the addresses and phone numbers of the Native entities, we include a brief discussion of the Alaska Native Claims Settlement Act of 1971 (ANCSA) and its key components, as well as brief descriptions of the various Alaska Native ethnic groups. Maps are included for each region to show village locations, and there is a statewide Native cultural map and a statewide Native regional corporation map. In this new edition, we also have added mission statements for many of the villages, corporations, and nonprofit organizations, and where possible, we have added traditional Native names for villages and communities.

The uses for this book will be as varied as visitors' and Alaskans' need for information. Alaska Natives seeking information on scholarships can look through the Alaska Native Education Consortium list, businesses partnering with Native corporations can learn about the history of ANCSA, and people seeking information about Native cultural heritage can find the nearest Native culture center. If you know only the name of a corporation or council, you can find the village listing for it in the index, then look up the address in the directory.

Those who have used this book in the past will notice that we have reorganized and expanded our listings in the hopes that they will be even more useful and convenient than previously. I am grateful to Veldee Hall, our editor, for tackling the task of updating and revising this edition. As with our other publications, we are pleased to inform you that proceeds from the sale of this book go toward scholarships and cultural programs of The CIRI Foundation.

Susan A. Anderson
President & CEO, The CIRI Foundation

Acknowledgements

A work of this nature does not come together without a tremendous team effort. Hallie and I are grateful to so many people and organizations for their help in making this book a reality. The person we need to thank first and foremost is Susan A. Anderson, President & CEO of The CIRI Foundation, who had the vision to suggest that we produce this book. We are also grateful to our supervisor, Sophie Minich, for all her support. Our original plan had been to create a pamphlet listing the names and addresses of the various entities in our Alaska Native History Database. It was Susan who suggested that we take our project to the next level and provide people with an inexpensive, small reference that would be of great value to tourists on even a short visit to Alaska, as well as those who live here.

Hallie has been gathering names and addresses in the Directory for nearly four years. During this time, she has been greatly assisted by all Native regional and village corporations, as well as traditional/IRA councils. Also assisting us have been the Alaska Federation of Natives, the First Alaskans Institute, The Aleut Foundation, Alutiiq Museum & Archaeological Repository, Bering Straits Foundation, Totem Heritage Center, Alaska Native Language Center, Sealaska Heritage Institute, Alaska Native Heritage Center, Chris Arend Photography, Alaska Pacific University, and the North Slope Borough, Planning Department, Commission of the Inupiat History, Language and Culture Division.

We also thank Wanetta Ayers, Alberta Stephan, Aaron Leggett, Alan Boraas, Tom Alton, Victoria Lord, Angela Bourdukofsky, Saunders McNeil, Debra Bissett, Charmaine Forbes, Amy Steffian, George Irvin, Carl Marrs, Christopher Savok, Paneen Petersen, Karen Tessandore, Chris Arend, Vera Metcalfe, John Johnson, Rosita Worl, Connie Irrigoo, Cindy Allred, Vicki Otte, Jan Seay, Bruce Hilton, Brianna Magby, Mike Irwin, Tony Vaska, and Roy Iutzi-Mitchell.

We also make special mention of Amanda L. Rothbarth, our graphic designer, and Crystal Rice, our proofreader. And we are grateful for the contributions of Chester Murphy and Daniel Martinez who worked so patiently on the Native region maps for the book.

Alexandra J. McClanahan
Hallie L. Bissett

Acknowledgements from the 2008 edition: As editor I would like to thank Hal Gage for graphic design, Blake Kowal for the updated maps, Jennifer Hoogendorn and Gretchen Sagan for project support. Special thanks to all the businesses and organizations that participated in this updated and expanded edition of Na'eda. And of course, A.J. McClanahan and Susan Anderson for bringing me into this project.

Veldee Hall

Table Of Contents

For Nick Gray...

"It has been my dream for many years that the Alaska Native would be organized to be an important political and economical and social force in our whole social structure."

—Nick Gray
Statewide Native Conference, October 19, 1966

The Alaska Native Claims Settlement Act

Alaska's indigenous people have carved their own cultures into an act of Congress that was an experiment in capitalism. In so doing, Alaska Natives have created successful business entities that differ from traditional Western business enterprises in significant ways. In addition, Native people have begun a process of developing enduring institutions that provide important services to Alaska Natives. Some of these may well long outlast the business enterprises that have made them possible.

"The white man come in and he took over land in secret. Nobody told us."

— Simon Paneak
written testimony, July 12, 1968

Alaska's economy and history continue to be dramatically affected by groundbreaking legislation signed by President Nixon on December 18, 1971. The Alaska Native Claims Settlement Act was a profound change in U.S. policy when it was passed, and the act itself has been significantly changed in its 30 years of life.

Byron Mallott, President & CEO of the First Alaskans Institute, has said that the experience of Native corporations created under the Alaska Native Claims Settlement Act, known as ANCSA, is an "epic story benefiting Alaska and all of its people."

Today, it is very difficult to imagine Alaska's economic and social landscape before ANCSA. That is due in part to the fact that passage of the act was a very positive step, and one that was a dramatic shift from decades of discrimination and policies seemingly designed to break the spirit of Alaska's First Peoples.

By the time non-Natives began arriving in Alaska, indigenous civilizations were spread across Alaska's vast reaches. Their cultures reached back for thousands of years. The first people to feel the effects of contact with the outside world were the Tlingits and the Aleuts. The effect of the invading Russians on the Aleuts beginning in the mid-1700s was devastating. For most of the rest of the people living in Alaska, contact was relatively limited until Alaska's purchase from Russia by the United States in 1867. Through the decades, however, non-Natives pressed into Alaska's most remote regions, increasing pressure on vital subsistence resources and putting greater numbers of people over the years at greater risk of not having enough food.

Adding even more stress to the indigenous populations, successive waves of disease ranging from smallpox to influenza wiped out thousands of people and, in some cases, entire communities. These began with first contact and continued on through the 1900s.

Western policies added another dimension to the difficulties. Both the missionaries and the federal education system for Natives had encouraged people, many of whom had traversed the wide, open spaces as nomadic bands, to settle into permanent enclaves. Although many of these villages were traditional gathering places, remaining in one place throughout the year made it much more difficult to obtain the life-sustaining fish and game food sources.

In 1924, Congress made citizens of all American Indians, including Alaska Natives. In the same year, Tlingit attorney William L. Paul became the first Alaska Native elected to serve in the Territorial Legislature. Paul and other Southeastern Alaska Natives eventually picked up the banner of Alaska Native land claims.

In his speech to the Alaska Native Brotherhood in 1977, Native rights champion Roy Peratrovich noted that it was during the Alaska Native Brotherhood-Alaska Native Sisterhood conventions of the 1920s that land claims were brought to the attention of Alaska Natives in Southeast Alaska. And they achieved at least a modicum of success.

In 1935, Congress passed a special act allowing the Tlingit and Haida Indians to bring suit on their claims against the United States for the lands taken from them. They then spent decades pursuing a lawsuit against the United States that stemmed from the 1907 appropriation of a large area of land in Southeast for the Tongass National Forest. In spite of such a glimmer of hope, there were few improvements in the social standing of Alaska Natives. When Roy and his wife Elizabeth moved in 1941 to Juneau, Alaska's capital city, they were stunned to find signs in front of businesses stating "We cater to White Trade only." In another place, they saw "No

Natives Allowed," and "No Dogs or Indians Allowed." The Peratroviches sought help from then Territorial Governor Ernest Gruening, who did what he could as far as asking individual proprietors to remove such signs. The Peratroviches realized that they needed to seek legislation to correct the situation, so they helped develop the Anti-Discrimination bill that was introduced in the Territorial Legislature during the 1943 session and was narrowly defeated that year.

The bill was finally passed in 1945, but not before vocal opposition from several senators, including personal attacks on the Peratroviches. An account of the exchange between Elizabeth Peratrovich and one of the senators is included in the book *Haa Kusteeyi, Our Culture: Tlingit Life Stories*. According to the book, Senator Allen Shattuck argued that the races should be kept farther apart, saying, "Who are these people, barely out of savagery, who want to associate with us whites with 5,000 years of recorded civilization behind us?"

Elizabeth Peratrovich responded: "I would not have expected that I, who am barely out of savagery, would have to remind gentlemen with 5,000 years of recorded civilization behind them of our Bill of Rights. When my husband and I came to Juneau and sought a home in a nice neighborhood where our children could play happily with our neighbor's children, we found such a house and arranged to lease it. When the owners learned that we were Indians, they said no. Would we be compelled to live in the slum?"

The situation in Juneau is only one example of the discrimination that took place against Native people. In Nome, Natives were expected to move aside if they encountered a white person coming toward them on the street. There, too, as in many other communities, Natives were relegated to a specific section of movie theaters.

Pressure on villages mounted greatly in the early 1960s with proposals for projects throughout the state that brought even greater numbers of non-Natives into Alaska. Among them were roads in Interior Alaska and a scheme called "Project Chariot" to blast a harbor near Point Hope with nuclear devices. Writing in the book *The Alaska Pipeline*, Mary Clay Berry discussed plans by the state to sell land claimed by Tanacross Natives near Lake George at the New York World's Fair of 1964. Claus-M.

Naske's *A History of the 49th State* discussed the stunning Rampart Dam, a proposal to build a dam 530 feet high and 4,700 feet long at the Rampart Canyon on the Yukon River. The dam would have put "the entire Yukon Flats—a vast network of sloughs, marshes and potholes that is one of the greatest wildfowl breeding grounds in North America—under several hundred feet of water." Seven villages with a total population of 1,200 people would have been flooded, according to Naske.

"...land and the Indians were bound together by ties of kinship and nature rather than by an understanding of property ownership. This conception is the very essence of Indian life..."

—Charles Etok Edwardsen, Jr.
written testimony, July 12, 1968

In their continuing efforts to protect their lands, Interior Athabascans raised concerns about non-Native incursion in the region. Naske describes how Stevens Village Natives sought to gain their lands and were among those opposing the Rampart Dam. Tanacross Village Natives filed claims for their lands in the 1940s. In 1961, the Regional Solicitor of the Department of the Interior issued an opinion in which he asserted that "Indian title" was involved in a protest by the Natives of Minto, Northway, Tanacross and Lake Alegnagik. This was in reaction to state plans to establish a recreation area near the Athabascan village of Minto and to construct a road into the area to make it accessible to Fairbanks residents. The people of Minto eventually hired Ted Stevens, the man who would become U.S. Senator for Alaska and eventually one of the most powerful senators in the nation. He offered his services free, according to Naske.

In 1964, many Inupiat joined together to form Inupiat Paitot to fight the proposed Project Chariot. Howard Rock, who was originally from Point Hope but had moved out of Alaska, returned to the state and founded the

Tundra Times, Alaska's first and only statewide Alaska Native newspaper. The newspaper greatly aided the Eskimos in their fight against the nuclear project, and they eventually were successful in halting it.

By the 1960s, the effort to push Alaska Natives to the sidelines of their own state had become too much to tolerate. Native groups throughout the state united to fight for their land, and they were joined by a number of non-Natives who decried the marginalization of an entire group of people. Before the decade of the 1960s had ended, Alaska Natives had officially filed claims to nearly the entire 375 million acres within Alaska, and the Alaska Federation of Natives (AFN) had mounted a full-scale effort to gain title to Native lands. At the same time, state officials were filing claims to some of the Alaska Natives' most important lands because the state had been granted 104 million acres under the Alaska Statehood Act of 1958.

Late in 1966, Interior Secretary Stewart Udall initiated a "land freeze" that was a moratorium on the process of conveying state land selections in order to preserve the status of Alaskan lands until the Native claims were settled. When vast oil reserves were discovered at Prudhoe Bay in 1968, developers and state officials were unwavering in the fight to lift the freeze.

By 1966 when the freeze was instituted by Udall, three critical pieces had to be put together in the fight for passage of the Alaska Native Claims Settlement Act: a statewide organization, money, and a statement that clearly articulated the issue.

- The organization—the dream of Inupiaq Nick Gray who worked tirelessly to organize Alaska Natives throughout the state—became the Alaska Federation of Natives.
- The money was provided in part by the Native Village of Tyonek when villagers shared some of their oil lease funds.
- The statement was a paper written by Willie Hensley from Kotzebue who explained why Alaska Natives had rights to—and not just a need for—their lands.

Without the generous financial assistance of the Native Village of Tyonek, the Alaska Federation of Natives would have been hard-pressed to gather Native people together from throughout the state. The village made a grant of $150,000 to AFN, as well as a loan of $100,000.

Hensley's paper tracked the historical and legal trail of Alaska Native land claims. In it, he detailed the legal situation facing Alaska Natives at that point and discussed laws that had been enacted after Alaska was purchased from Russia by the United States. The paper was responsible for helping to educate non-Native Alaskans and those in the Lower 48 about Alaska Natives' rights, as well as putting Native claims into perspective for many Alaska Natives. It was titled: "What Rights to Land Have the Alaskan Natives?"

Joseph H. Fitzgerald, former chairman of the Federal Field Committee, which developed a massive landmark publication that detailed the plight of Alaska Natives in 1968, favored settling land claims. And the publication Fitzgerald's committee developed, *Alaska Natives and the Land*, showed that from a Western viewpoint, Alaska Natives were fighting from ground zero. In 1968, Alaska Natives owned less than 500 acres in fee simple title and held only an additional 15,000 acres in restricted title. The study noted that some 900 Native families shared the use of 4 million acres of land in 23 reserves established for their use and administered by the Bureau of Indian Affairs. All other rural Native families at the time lived on the public domain.

Alaska Natives' urgent task in the face of the State of Alaska beginning its selection of land was to protect as much land as they could and make sure that it remained under Native control. Their aim was to give up as little as possible while maintaining as much traditional land as they could.

Although there was disagreement over what was to be accomplished by settling the claims, there was little debate about the situation Natives faced at the time. Throughout several years of hearings, witness after witness talked about terrible conditions in rural Alaska. In 1968, a number of witnesses compared conditions in many of the villages to Appalachia. But former Attorney General John Rader testified that even that comparison didn't go far enough.

"I noticed that they said in the Appalachia testimony—they said that the lack of adequate sewage treatment facilities turned some of the great assets of Appalachia into liabilities. The streams were polluted and so on and so forth. I was talking to a VISTA worker the other day and he said they did not have toilets, sewers, or even outhouses. The only trouble with the Appalachia comparison is that it is so mild," he testified before the Senate Committee on Interior and Insular Affairs.

An Athabascan raised in the Cook Inlet Region has described what it felt like to be an Alaska Native in the state in the late 1960s—before the Alaska Native Claims Settlement Act: "We were like foreigners in our own country."

Legislation was developed under intense pressures—most notably the desire for oil development, but also the state's push to get its 104 million acres. At the same time, there was a growing realization within the United States that Indian treaties of the past had mostly been a license to steal lands from the nation's aboriginal peoples. It was time to do something new.

"We are only asking for what has been ours for many generations"

—Bobby W. Esai, Sr.
written testimony, October 17-18, 1969

The proposals offered by Alaska Natives departed from past Indian policy. Rather than creating reservations, Alaska Natives were trying to craft a creative alternative to the reservation system in the Lower 48, which yoked people to the hulking bureaucracy of the Bureau of Indian Affairs. Rather than granting land and money to Indian governments, the legislation would set up business corporations to manage Native resources.

The corporate provisions of the proposed bill emerged mainly as what was left over when traditional ideas such as reservations were rejected. They were the only feasible alternative to the creation of a reservation system in the state.

In her written testimony offered to the House Subcommittee on Indian Affairs in 1969, Inupiaq Laura Bergt strongly supported the creation of corporations.

I believe it's extremely necessary for the regional corporation to control and manage our settlement funds. It's only reasonable that we should control and develop our resources from the settlement—and the most important one of all, the Alaskan Native. Who could be better qualified than we?

…I strongly urge you to weigh these factors and work towards vesting these powers to the regional corporation concept. This show of respect and confidence in the Alaskan Native will be truly appreciated besides showing wise judgment, understanding and faith in the Alaskan Native on your part. I'm confident that you will be extremely pleased with the capability, responsibility, and intelligence of the Alaska Native in managing his own affairs.

In 1971 the Natives' efforts paid off with what would become the Alaska Native Claims Settlement Act (ANCSA). For four long years, spirited debate had focused on just how much land and cash the Alaska Natives would be granted. The final bill that emerged promised 44 million acres and $1 billion in cash.

After Congress passed ANCSA, Alaska Natives gathered at the Alaska Methodist University for a special meeting called by Don Wright, who was originally from Nenana and served as President of the Alaska Federation of Natives during the final crucial year of lobbying. Gaining passage was a victory for the dozens of Alaska Natives who had spent countless hours in Washington, D.C., thousands of miles away from their homes. But when the gathering of Alaska Natives in Anchorage was informed of the news, the feeling at that time was more one of stunned resignation about what had been lost rather than excited elation over what had been retained.

With passage of the act, Congress took away most of Alaska Natives' land. Alaska Natives retained 44 million acres out of 375 million acres and were granted nearly $1 billion for lands given up. The money was paid out over a period of years. Natives owned their land fee simple title, which was a shift from the government's previous policy of granting land in a trust status with the U.S. Department of the Interior. While it meant that Natives could sell what was essentially their birthright, it also meant they would choose their own destiny without having to ask the federal government for "permission" to undertake economic activities. Although the total amount of cash granted sounded like a lot of money, it meant that Alaska Natives failed in their attempt to get an overriding royalty in perpetuity and that there was a cap on the funds to be received.

It's important to point out that while many in the non-Native community viewed ANCSA as a "generous" grant to Alaska Natives, what was given up overshadowed what was gained. As Wright had testified earlier in 1971 when he was urging the Senate to support a 60-million-acre bill: "We are not asking for anything. We are offering the U.S. Government 84 percent of our property. We are offering them … more than 300 million acres to satisfy the needs of others in the state and to satisfy the needs of the United States in the way of federal reserves, wildlife refuges, wilderness areas … We will accommodate them all. We are asking merely to be able to retain 16 percent of our land in each region and we are asking for extinguishment of titles to the other 300 million acres, $500 million from the Congress and 2 percent royalty in perpetuity which will be utilized over the whole state of Alaska."

In the end, the amount of land retained was about 10 percent, the cash was capped at $1 billion, and special protections for subsistence purposes were left hanging.

The fight for land claims required people to rise above their own personal needs and work with others despite differences in opinion and culture. Some of the Native leaders who worked closely together came from cultures that had traditionally been at odds with other Native cultures. They were united because the fight was an effort to end the victimization of thousands of people who wanted nothing more—and nothing less—than a better world for their children.

A number of Native leaders have noted that the act was an experiment on a grand scale, and it was a radical departure for Congress, which in the past had dealt with indigenous people with treaties that were eventually broken. And, of course, a key difference between a treaty and an act of Congress is that treaties are not altered over time, but acts can be amended whenever the need arises.

Thirty years ago it was Native ties to the land and a desire to control their own destiny that spurred Native leaders to make innumerable sacrifices to get ANCSA passed. Many Alaska Natives stepped forward to fight for their rights by sacrificing their time, their energy and their own financial resources. Non-Natives, as well, joined together with Alaska Natives to speak out in favor of a fair settlement of Alaska Native claims.

Today there are several hundred Native corporations, non-profit organizations, and other entities that are a direct result of ANCSA. ANCSA is not the basis for all Native organizations and entities, but a large number of them flowed out of ANCSA's passage. All of the ANCSA business enterprises and organizations form a very large, flowing tent. It is a tent that provides a great deal of shelter to many people. And its central lodgepole is ANCSA. While the act is critical in holding up the entire tent, its strength rests in how firmly it is anchored in Alaska. Alaska is the landscape where countless cultural beliefs and traditions are nurtured.

What makes Native corporations so different from other business enterprises is that they concern themselves with the "real economic and social needs of Natives." These very words were at the heart of what ANCSA was in 1971 and remain so to this day. There have been many strides in improving the lives of Alaska Natives in every part of the state; still, many people continue to deal with serious problems.

As it was passed, ANCSA had major structural flaws, and the Native leadership knew it. It was just vague enough that government officials almost got away with trying to unravel it in its early years of implementation. It contained a 20-year "time bomb" because it called for Natives to be allowed to sell the stock in their Native corporations after 1991. It required Native corporations to share resource revenues with each other, but failed to detail how that would be accomplished. It forced a Western system of individual rights on tribal peoples. Over the next three decades, the Native leadership had no choice but to deal with each of these issues.

While many compelling chapters of the story have been written over its 30-year history to address these problems, it may be that some of the most exciting events have yet to be recorded.

An Overview Of ANCSA

*The people affected by the act, its structure, how
money was distributed, and how land was conveyed.*

Stella Martin is a Tlingit elder from Kake in Southeast Alaska who was
born in 1922. Her uncle, Frank Johnson, was an important early advocate
for Native rights, and she recalls just how difficult it was for a group of
people who were basically impoverished to scrounge up enough cash
to send him out to speak on their behalf. In an interview, she recalled a
time when she was a child that her father wanted her mother to go get the
emergency money they had been saving:

> *My father came to my mother, and he said, "You know that money that
> we were saving?" He said, "We're going to have to give it to Frank
> because he's going to Washington, D.C."*
>
> *My mother started to cry. She didn't say anything, but she turned.
> And when she came back, she had two one-dollar bills that were folded
> so tight. That was the emergency money. She gave it to him. She was
> still crying, and I wondered why she was crying because as a small
> child, I didn't understand.*
>
> *Two dollars just seems like a small amount right now, but at the time
> it was a lot of money. It was all the money they had.*

The Alaska Native Claims Settlement Act is a very complex document
that has inspired people over the last three decades to write thousands
of pages about it. The Act, known as ANCSA, has been praised, and it
has been roundly criticized. But what's really important to keep in mind
when discussing ANCSA is that it is a document that was developed for a
group of human beings who had a very real claim to their ancestral home
in Alaska. Their connection to the land is a spiritual one that transcends
complex regulatory schemes.

People

There were nearly 80,000 Alaska Natives alive on December 18, 1971,
who could participate in the Alaska Native Claims Settlement Act. Most of
those affected by the Act were in Alaska, but about 20,000 people lived in
the Lower 48 and even other parts of the world.

"Native" was defined as a citizen of the United States with one-fourth degree or more Indian, Aleut or Eskimo ancestry, born on or before December 18, 1971, including Natives who had been adopted by one or more non-Native parents. All Alaska Natives alive on the effective date through enrollment became eligible to be shareholders in the new corporations. Amendments were passed later to allow Native corporations to issue stock to those born after December 18, 1971.

Structure

The corporate structure of ANCSA was a departure for Congress. Corporations, not reservations, were organized to administer the proceeds from the historical land claims settlement for Alaska Natives.

Thirteen regional corporations, including 12 in Alaska and one that was created later to represent Alaska Natives living outside the state, were authorized. Alaska Natives who enrolled were made shareholders when they received 100 shares of stock. The size of the regional corporations ranged from Ahtna, Inc., with about 1,000 shareholders, to Sealaska Corporation, with about 16,000 shareholders. Others included: The Aleut Corporation; Arctic Slope Regional Corporation; Bering Straits Native Corporation; Bristol Bay Native Corporation; Calista Corporation; Chugach Alaska Corporation; Cook Inlet Region, Inc.; Doyon, Limited; Koniag, Inc.; NANA Regional Corporation, Inc.; and the Thirteenth Regional Corporation.

Approximately 220 village corporations were created under ANCSA, and villages were given a choice as to whether they wanted to incorporate as profit or non-profit entities. None chose to be non-profit. The reason for this is that the corporations were founded under state law which didn't allow non-profits to pay distributions to members. A profit corporation, however, was authorized to pay dividends to shareholders.

Alaska Natives who enrolled to their village received 100 shares of village corporation stock. Those who elected not to enroll in a village corporation, but enrolled in a regional corporation were called "at-large" shareholders. There was a lot of confusion over enrollment, but generally speaking, Alaska Natives were allowed to enroll to the region and village where they grew up and which they considered home or to the region where they were living at the time the act was passed.

The size of villages ranged from 25 people to about 2,000. The larger village corporations, each of which included about 2,000 people, were Barrow, Nome, Bethel and Kotzebue. A few corporations have used amendments passed to the act to create a new class of stock for those born after Dec. 18, 1971. In general, this has been done through the creation of a new type of stock, known as "life estate stock." This stock is valid only during the shareholder's lifetime and cannot be passed on.

Amendments passed in 1976 authorized village corporations to merge with each other or with their regional corporations. Some villages have merged, such as The Kuskokwim Corporation in the Calista Region; MTNT, Ltd., Gana-A'Yoo, Ltd., and K'oytl'ots'ina, Ltd., in the Doyon Region; the Alaska Peninsula Corporation and Choggiung, Ltd., in the Bristol Bay Region; and Afognak Native Corporation and Akhiok-Kaguyak Inc. in the Koniag Region.

All the villages in the Ahtna Region except Chitina merged with Ahtna; all the villages in the NANA Region except Kotzebue merged with NANA; and Karluk merged with Koniag.

At least two villages distributed their assets to the village tribal government, and that was done by Venetie and Arctic Village.

The structure has become the source of heated debate for many years. One of the more powerful statements that has been made about ANCSA was offered by the senator who more than anyone else can take credit for the act's final provisions. Senator Henry "Scoop" Jackson, Chairman of the Senate Interior and Insular Affairs Committee at the time of the passage of ANCSA, talked about the tension that existed between the notion of Western-style corporations and Native cultural needs in his keynote address to AFN in 1981:

"This is a debate which I have watched for the past thirteen years. It is a debate for which there are no ultimate answers. At one time, I thought it was a serious mistake to mix social welfare objectives with the traditional Corporation's more limited objective of maximizing profitability. Today, I must confess to having changed my mind. The Regional Corporations are totally unique. Their performance cannot be measured by gross revenue and net profit standards alone. Judgments about their performance must be made on the basis of total performance in the achievement of shareholder goals."

Money

The amount of money distributed through ANCSA was $962 million, which was essentially determined on a per capita basis. It came from both the State of Alaska and the Federal Government over a period of about 11 years. The long time frame for distribution greatly diminished its value due to inflation. In the first five years, 10 percent of the money distributed went to all individuals who were shareholders. The regions retained 45 percent of the total, and the remaining 45 percent was distributed to the villages and the "at-large" shareholders on a per capita basis. (At-large shareholders were those who enrolled only to a region and not a village.)

After the first five years, the money was distributed 50-50 with half retained by the regional corporations and half distributed to the village corporations and at-large shareholders on a per capita basis.

A provision of ANCSA, Section 7(i), requires that regional corporations share 70 percent of their resource revenues from their ANCSA lands among the corporations. Under Section 7(j), half of the money each region receives through 7(i) is shared with their villages and at-large shareholders on a per capita basis.

The sharing provision is an extremely unusual aspect of ANCSA and it took the corporations about 10 years to hammer out an agreement that spelled out exactly how this would be undertaken. The concept was sound—find a way to make sure that resource-rich corporations shared with those who were resource-poor simply by accident of location. But once lawyers and accountants got involved in the implementation, it nearly broke the bonds holding Native groups together. Only after the Native leadership took control of the issue themselves was it resolved in a harmonious manner.

As Byron Mallott, one of the early leaders who lobbied for ANCSA has said, "Seven (i) was easy to put in the Act because none of us were business people. What if in the airline industry all airlines had to share 70 percent of their revenues, one with the other, because the government believed there should be equity in air transportation?"

"If we'd known business or had any business experience, particularly on the finance side, someone would have posed the fairly straightforward and obvious question: Well, shouldn't we define 'revenue' in the Act? It seemed simple and elegant as public policy and became very, very difficult in its implementation."

Land

The land conveyed under ANCSA was 44 million acres, which was a little more than 10 percent of the entire state. It sounds like a tremendous amount of land, especially when compared to treaties the United States made earlier with American Indians. When viewed as what was granted to the people who had a valid claim to the entire state, however, the settlement seems relatively small.

Of the 44 million acres, 22 million acres of surface estate went to village corporations on a formula based on population. This land was generally located around the village itself and consisted of prime subsistence areas. The subsurface estate of this land went to the regional corporations. Sixteen million acres went to the regional corporations, and that included both the surface and the subsurface estate; and two million acres was conveyed for specific situations, such as cemeteries, historical sites, and villages with fewer than 25 people. Another four million acres went to former reserves where the villages took land instead of land and money. These former reserves were granted land entitlements ranging from 700,000 to 2 million acres. They included Gambell and Savoonga on St. Lawrence Island, Elim, Tetlin, and Venetie and Arctic Village. Klukwan originally opted for this provision, but leaders there later changed their minds.

Not affected by the ANCSA was Metlakatla on Annette Island in Southeast Alaska, established in 1891. Metlakatla was a reservation before ANCSA, and remained one afterwards.

All the leaders' efforts were focused on the land. As Trefon Angasan, Vice President of Shareholder and Corporate Relations of Bristol Bay Native Corporation, has said: "When the concept of Natives fighting for their land came about—we just assumed that it was our land. Because no one had ever said anything that it wasn't. We looked out into the open space and said, Hey, this is Native land. This is our land. It was always there: that sense of ownership of it was always there. And, then all of a sudden, in the late '60s, they were beginning to draw boundaries around it, and you began to realize that the world was changing."

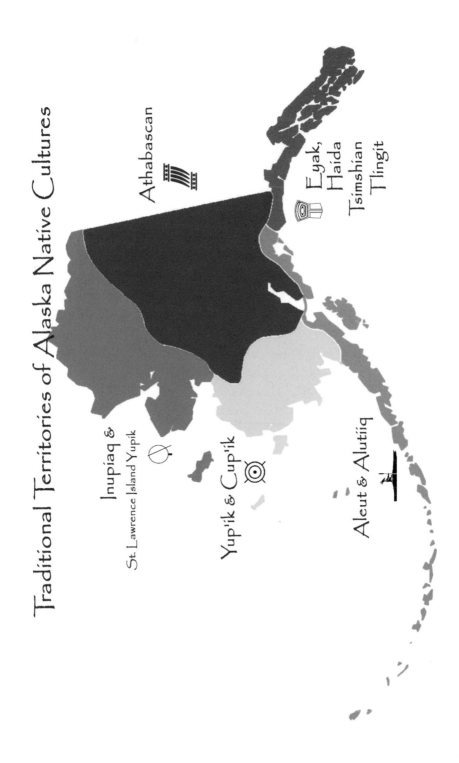

Traditional Territories of Alaska Native Cultures

Athabascan

Eyak, Haida
Tsimshian
Tlingit

Inupiaq &
St. Lawrence Island Yupik

Yup'ik & Cup'ik

Aleut & Alutiiq

Cultural Groups Of Alaska

Aleut/Alutiiq

Aleut

The Unangas (Aleut people) inhabited the Aleutian Islands several thousand years ago, well before European explorers arrived. Rough, windy seas surround these remote, rocky, majestically beautiful, volcanic islands; people living there experience some of the most inclement weather in the world.

Despite the tempestuous surroundings, the Unangas adapted to the environment and became excellent navigators of the sea, skillfully harvesting its unlimited bounties as their main livelihood. They were designers and craftsmen of sea vessels called "baidarkas" which are well known for excellent maneuverability over the ocean no matter what weather conditions prevailed.

The Aleut Corporation

Alutiiq

The foggy spruce forests, windswept coastal meadows, and mountainous rocky fjords of the central Gulf of Alaska are the traditional homeland of the Alutiit. Archaeological data indicate that they have lived in this region for more than 7,500 years. Also known as the Sugpiat—an Alutiiq term meaning real people, or the Aleut—a Russian term meaning coastal dweller, the Alutiit share deep ancestral ties with Alaska's Eskimo and Unangan people. A maritime culture, the Alutiit have always made their living from the sea.

Large whaling villages and fishing communities governed by wealthy chiefs once harvested marine mammals, fish, birds and shellfish to feed their families and manufacture all the objects of daily life. Contact with outsiders in the past 200 years—Russians, Scandinavians, Americans, and Asians—has altered the fabric of the Alutiiq culture. However, an Alutiiq way of interacting with the world still thrives. There are more than 4,000 Alutiit today, and like their ancestors, many continue to make a living from the sea.

Amy Steffian, deputy director Alutiiq Museum and Archeological Repository

Note: *Alutiiq is the singular and the adjective—for example, an Alutiiq person, Alutiiq heritage. Alutiit is the plural—for example, Alutiit live on the coast, Chugach Alutiit collected berries in the fall.*

Chugach

Archeological evidence shows that the Chugach people have survived and prospered for thousands of years. Oldest legends tell of the last ice age when Prince William Sound was largely covered by glaciers. Three major Alaska Native cultures—Eskimo, Indian, and Aleut have inhabited the region.

Although it is not known how long people have occupied the region, archeological finds indicate a 6,000-year habitation on Kodiak and Afognak islands.

The migration of the people has not been firmly established. Their language, Alutiiq, is closely related to the Yup'ik of the central Bering Sea people.

John Johnson, *Chugach Legends*

Yup'ik/Cup'ik

Central Alaskan Yup'ik is the largest of the state's Native languages, both in the size of its population and the number of speakers. Of a total population of about 21,000 people, about 10,000 are speakers of the language. Children still grow up speaking Yup'ik as their first language in 17 of 68 Yup'ik villages, those mainly located on the lower Kuskokwim River, on Nelson Island, and along the coast between the Kuskokwim River and Nelson Island. The main dialect is General Central Yup'ik, and the other four dialects are Norton Sound, Hooper Bay-Chevak, Nunivak, and Egegik. In the Hooper Bay-Chevak and Nunivak dialects, the name for the language and the people is Cup'ik (pronounced Chup-pik).

The Alaska Native Language Center

Inupiaq/St. Lawrence Island Yupik

Inupiaq

The name Inupiaq, meaning real or genuine person (inuk: person, and -piaq: real, genuine), is often spelled Iñupiaq, particularly in the northern dialects. It can refer to a person of this group (he is an Inupiaq) and can also be used as an adjective (she is an Inupiaq woman). The plural form of the noun is Inupiat, referring to the people collectively (the Inupiat of the North Slope). The Alaska Native Language Center

Alaska is home to about 13,500 Inupiat. About 3,000, most of whom are over age 40, speak the language.

Creativity and flexibility, knowledge about the environment, and survival skills continue to be important elements of modern Inupiaq culture. Hunting, especially whaling, remains central to people's lives today. Although much of the hunting technology has changed, the Inupiat of Barrow continue to rely upon traditional knowledge for successful hunting. Skin boats are still used for spring whaling. Navigation skills and understanding animal behavior are still required of a successful hunter.

North Slope Borough, Planning Department,
Commission of the Inupiat History, Language & Culture Division, Barrow, Alaska

St. Lawrence Island Yupik (Siberian Yupik)

Siberian Yupik is spoken in the two St. Lawrence Island villages of Gambell and Savoonga. The language of St. Lawrence Island is nearly identical to the language spoken across the Bering Strait on the tip of the Siberian Chukchi Peninsula. The total Siberian Yupik population in Alaska is about 1,100, and of that number about 1,050 speak the language. Children in both Gambell and Savoonga still learn Siberian Yupik as the first language of the home. Of a population of about 900 Siberian Yupik people in Siberia, there are about 300 speakers, although no children learn it as their first language.

The Alaska Native Language Center

Note: *The use of the apostrophe in Central Alaskan Yup'ik as opposed to Siberian Yupik denotes a long p. (Yup'ik is pronounced Yup-pik, and Cup'ik is pronounced Chup-pik).*

Athabascan

There are 11 Athabascan languages spoken by 11 regional bands within Alaska. According to the Alaska Native Language Center at the University of Alaska Fairbanks, these include: Ahtna, Dena'ina (Tanaina), Deg Xinag (Ingalik), Holikachuk, Upper Kuskokwim, Koyukon, Tanana, Tanacross, Upper Tanana, Gwich'in (Kutchin), and Hän.

Athabascans followed similar patterns in their subsistence activities, although each regional band utilized different food sources. According to the Alaska Native Knowledge Network, the general pattern consisted of fishing in the summer and fall, hunting caribou and moose in the fall, trapping water mammals in the spring, and harvesting vegetable foods in the spring, summer, and fall.

Eyak/Tlingit/Haida/Tsimshian

Eyak

The Eyak Nation is now small in number. Their last stronghold was in the Cordova area. They are related to the Athabascans but are not Athabascans. It was reported that they migrated down the Copper River to the shores of the Prince William Sound; however this route is not known for sure.

The Eyaks must have originally been inland people. They migrated to the ocean and coexisted with the two powerful maritime nations of the Chugach and the Tlingit. Upon reaching this new land, the Eyaks had to either fight, retreat or join forces. They lived and fought together with their Tlingit Indian neighbors and did battle mainly against the Chugach. This led to Eyaks slowly being assimilated by the Tlingits and thus learning two languages. The Eyaks and Tlingits lived together in villages from Cordova to Yakutat. This blending of cultures worked well, since both cultures were socially organized with the clan system of the Eagle and Raven.

John Johnson, *Eyak Legends of the Copper River Delta*

Tlingit

Tlingit Indians live in Southeast Alaska from Yakutat to Dixon Entrance, predominantly on the coast, but with inland communities along the Chilkat and Stikine rivers in Alaska, and in Southwest Yukon and Northwest British Columbia.

Coastal Tlingits live in and on the edge of the rainforest—the most extensive temperate rainforest in the world, reaching from Puget Sound to Kodiak Island. This environment has shaped their lifestyle and material culture, along with those of other cultures of the Northwest Coast.

Haa Kusteeyi, *Tlingit Life Stories*

Haida

Haida is the language of the southern half of Prince of Wales Island in the villages of Hydaburg, Kasaan, and Craig, as well as a portion of the city of Ketchikan. About 600 Haida people live in Alaska, and about 15 of the most elderly among them speak the language. Haida is considered a linguistic isolate with no proven genetic relationship to any language family.

The Alaska Native Language Center

Tsimshian

Originally from Canada, the Tsimshian people now inhabit Alaska's only Indian reservation, Metlakatla. The reservation was founded in 1887 by a group of Tsimshians who came from Prince Rupert, British Columbia. According to the Alaska Native Language Center, of the 1,300 Tsimshian people living in Alaska today, not more than 70 of the most elderly speak the language.

Southeast Nations' Moieties & Marriage

The Tlingit, Haida and Tsimshian societies are matrilineal. That is, they trace their descent through the mother's line. The moiety is a social division that traditionally regulates marriage. A member of the Haida and Tlingit nation belongs to either the Eagle-Wolf or Raven moiety. The Tsimshian people are divided into four groups: Wolf, Killer Whale or Bear, Eagle, and Raven.

Under this system, children must marry into the opposite moiety. For example, in traditional Haida or Tlingit society, a person of the Eagle moiety could only marry someone of the opposite Raven moiety. Today the marriage rules are much more relaxed.

Ketchikan Museums

12 Regional Corporations created under ANCSA

BERIN
STRAIT

CALIS

ALEUT

ARCTIC SLOPE

ANA

DOYON

COOK
INLET AHTNA

STOL
AY

CHUGACH

SEALASKA

KONIAG

State of Alaska

50 0   100   200

Approximate Statute Miles

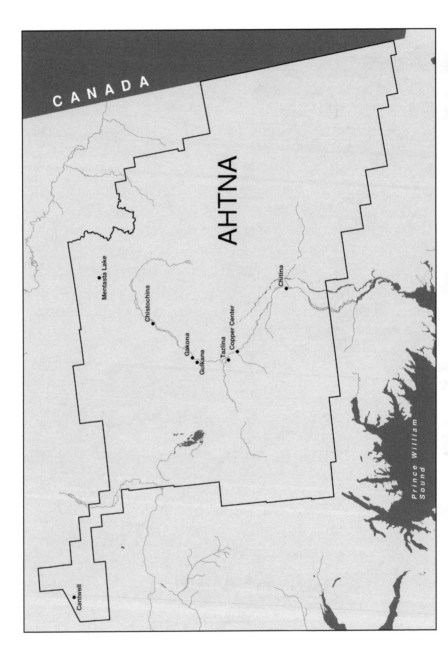

Ahtna, Incorporated

P.O. Box 649
Glennallen, AK 99588
Office (907) 822-3476
Fax (907) 822-3495
www.ahtna-inc.com

Mission: Ahtna, Inc., a growth-oriented company, will enhance the overall well-being of its shareholders with monetary dividends, employment and educational opportunities through diversified investments, and support a strong sense of cultural pride and identity. Ahtna will implement ANCSA for the benefit of its shareholders through the wise stewardship of land and natural resources and through sustained growth for the future generations.

Ahtna Region Villages (*and Traditional Names*)

Cantwell
Chistochina (*Cheesh-Na*)
Chitina
Copper Center (*Kluti-Kaah*)
Gakona
Gulkana
Mentasta Lake (*Mentasta*)
Tazlina

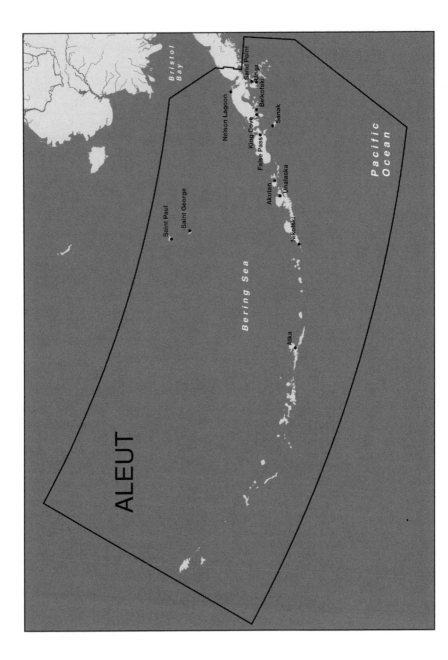

The Aleut Corporation

4000 Old Seward Highway, Suite 300
Anchorage, AK 99503
Office (907) 561-4300
(800) 232-4882
Fax (907) 563-4328
Email: info@aleutcorp.com
www.aleutcorp.com

Mission: to maximize dividends to, and choices for, our shareholders.

Aleut Region Villages (*and Traditional Names*)

Akutan
Atka
Belkofski
False Pass
King Cove
Nelson Lagoon (*Agdaagux*)
Nikolski
St. George
St. Paul
Sanak
Sand Point (*Qagun Tayagungin*)
Unalaska
Unga

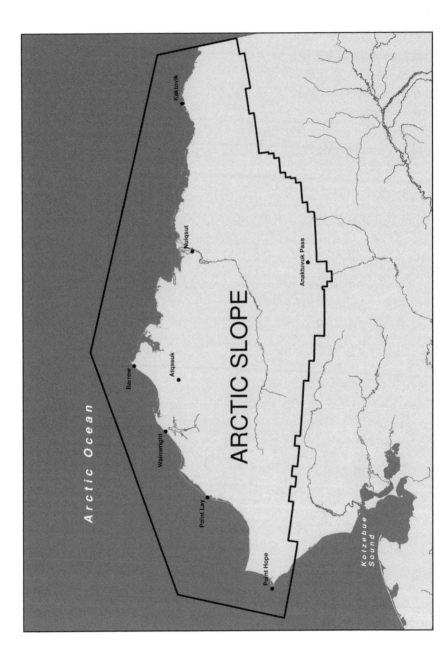

Arctic Slope Regional Corporation

3900 C Street, Suite 801
Anchorage, AK 99503-5963
Office (907) 339-6000
Fax (907) 339-6028
www.asrc.com

Mission: to actively manage our lands, resources, diversified operating subsidiaries, and investments throughout the world in order to enhance Inupiat cultural and economic freedoms.

Arctic Slope Region Villages (*and Traditional Names*)

Anaktuvuk Pass (*Anaqtuuvak)*
Atqasuk
Barrow (*Utqiabvik)*
Kaktovik (*Qaaktubvik)*
Nuiqsut (*Nuiqsat)*
Point Hope (*Tikibaq)*
Point Lay (*Kali)*
Wainwright (*Tikibaq)*

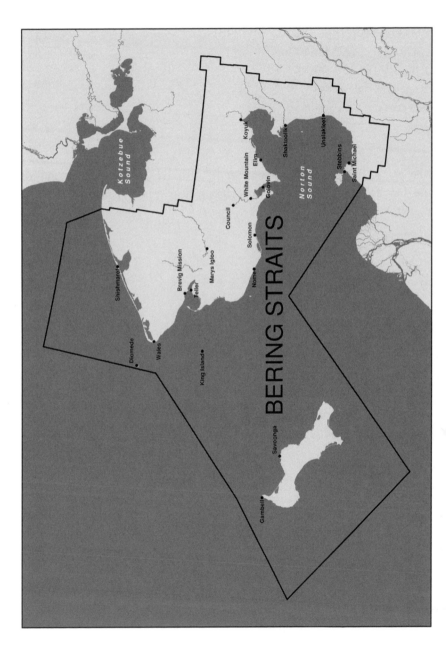

Bering Straits Native Corporation

P.O. Box 1008
Nome, AK 99762
Office (907) 443-5252
Fax (907) 443-2985
Email rose@beringstraits.com
www.beringstraits.com

Mission: to improve the quality of life of our people through economic development while protecting our land, and preserving our culture and heritage.

Bering Straits Region Villages (*and Traditional Names*)

Brevig Mission
Council
Diomede (*Inalik*)
Elim
Gambell (*Sivuqaq*)
Golovin (*Chinik*)
King Island (*Ukivok*)
Koyuk
Mary's Igloo
Nome
St. Michael
Savoonga
Shaktoolik
Shishmaref
Solomon

Stebbins
Teller
Unalakleet
Wales (*Kingigin*)
White Mountain (*Unga*)

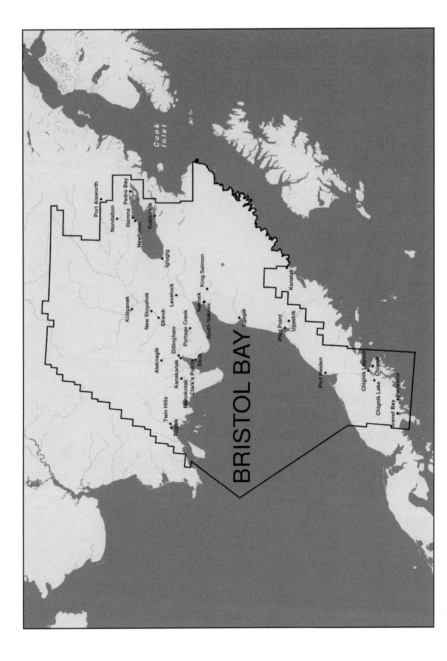

Bristol Bay Native Corporation

111 West 16th Avenue, Suite 400
Anchorage, AK 99501
Office (907) 278-3602
(800) 426-3602
Fax (907) 276-3925
www.bbnc.net

Mission: enriching our Native way of life.

Bristol Bay Region Villages (*and Traditional Names*)

Aleknagik
Chignik or Chignik Bay
Chignik Lagoon
Chignik Lake
Clark's Point
Dillingham (*Curyung*)
Egegik
Ekuk
Ekwok
Igiugig
Iliamna (*Nilavena*)
Ivanof Bay
Kanatak
King Salmon (*Sovonoski*)
Kokhanok (*Kakhanok*)
Koliganek

Levelock
Manokotak
Naknek
Newhalen
New Stuyahok
Nondalton
Pedro Bay
Perryville
Pilot Point
Port Alsworth (*Tanalian*)
Port Heiden (*Meshik*)
Portage Creek (*Ohgsenakale*)
South Naknek (*Qinuyang*)
Togiak
Twin Hills
Ugashik

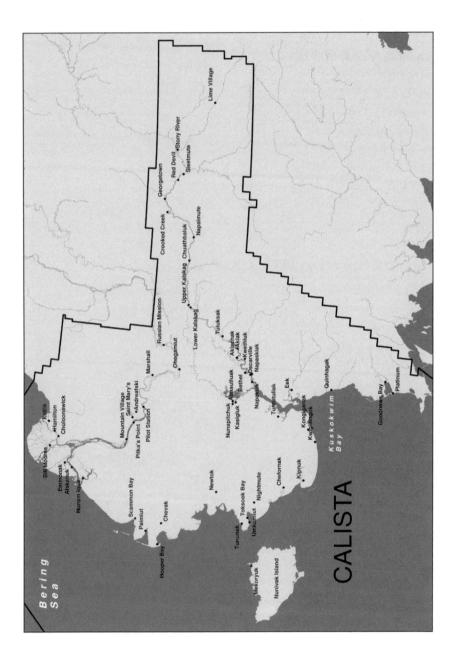

Calista Corporation

301 Calista Court, Suite A
Anchorage, AK 99518-3028
Office (907) 279-5516
Fax (907) 279-8430
Email calista@calistacorp.com
www.calistacorp.com

Mission: provides sound, progressive, business ventures which promote self-determination, and economic and social well-being that improves the quality of life for those we serve. Our success will be measured by increased regional employment, corporate profits, and shareholder benefits.

Calista Region Villages (*and Traditional Names*)

Akiachak	Kalskag (*Upper Kalskag*)	Ohogamiut
Akiak	Lower Kalskag (*Lower Kalskag*)	Oscarville (*Kuiggayagaq*)
Alakanuk	Kasigluk (*Kaseglok*)	Paimiut
Andreafski	Kipnuk (*Kanganak*)	Pilot Station
Aniak	Kongiganak (*Kong*)	Pitka's Point
Atmautluak	Kotlik	Platinum
Bethel (*Orutsararmuit*)	Kwethluk	Quinhagak (*Kwinhagak*)
Bill Moore's Slough	Kwigillingok (*Kwig*)	Red Devil
Chefornak (*Chefornok*)	Lime Village	Russian Mission
Chevak (*Kashunamiut*)	Marshall or Fortuna Ledge	St. Mary's (*Algaaciq*)
Chuathbaluk (*Russian Mission*)	Mekoryuk	Scammon Bay
Chuloonawick	Mountain Village (*Asa' Carsarmiut*)	Sheldon's Point (*Nunam Iqua*)
Crooked Creek	Napaimute	Sleetmute
Eek	Napakiak	Stony River
Emmonak	Napaskiak	Toksook Bay (*Nuna Kauyak*)
Georgetown	Newtok	Tuluksak (*Tananak*)
Goodnews Bay	Nightmute	Tuntutuliak (*Tunt*)
Hamilton	Nunapitchuk	Tununak
Hooper Bay (*Naparyarmiut*)	Nunivak Island	Umkumiut (*Umkumiute*)

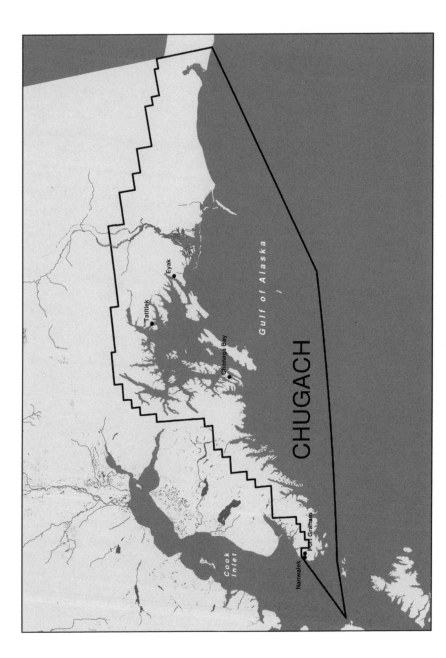

Chugach Alaska Corporation

561 East 36th Avenue
Anchorage, AK 99503
Office (907) 563-8866
Fax (907) 563-8402
www.chugach-ak.com

Mission: Chugach Alaska Corporation is committed to profitability, celebration of our heritage, and ownership of our lands.

Chugach Region Villages (*and Traditional Names*)

Chenega Bay
Eyak
English Bay (*Nanwalek*)
Port Graham (*Paluwik*)
Tatitlek

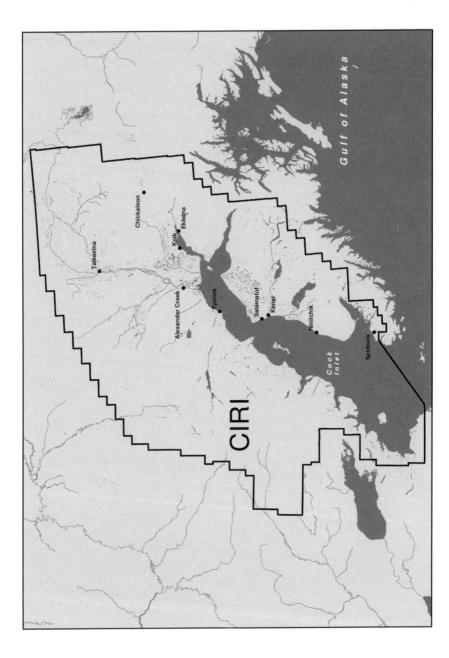

Cook Inlet Region, Inc.

P.O. Box 93330
Anchorage, AK 99509
Office (907) 274-8638
Fax (907) 263-5186
(800) 764-2474
www.ciri.com

Mission: our mission is to promote the economic and social well-being and Alaska Native Heritage of our shareholders, now and into the future, through prudent stewardship of the company's resources, while furthering self-sufficiency among CIRI shareholders and their families.

Cook Inlet Region Villages (and Traditional Names)

Alexander Creek (*Tuqen Kaq*)
Chickaloon (*Nay'dini'aa Na'*)
Eklutna (*Idlughet*)
Kenai (*Shk'ituk't*)
Knik (*K'enakatnu*)
Ninilchik (*Niqnalchint*)
Salamatof (*Ken Dech'Etl't*)
Seldovia (*Angidahtnu*)
Tyonek (*Tubghnenq*)

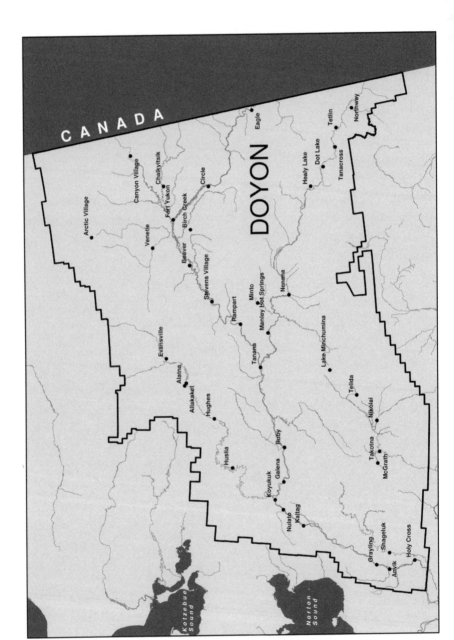

Doyon, Limited

1 Doyon Place, Suite 300
Fairbanks, AK 99701-2941
Office (907) 459-2000
Fax (907) 459-2060
(888) 478-4755
www.doyon.com

Mission: to continually enhance our position as a financially strong Native corporation in order to promote the economic and social well-being of our shareholders and future shareholders, to strengthen our Native way of life, and to protect and enhance our land and resources.

Doyon Region Villages (*and Traditional Names*)

Alatna	Galena (*Louden*)	Nenana
Allakaket (*New*	Grayling	Nikolai
Allakaket)	Healy Lake	(*Edzeno Nikolai*)
Anvik	Holy Cross	Northway
Arctic Village	Hughes	Nulato
Beaver	(*Hut'odleekkaakk'et*	Rampart
Birch Creek	*Tribe*)	Ruby
(*Dendu Gwich'in Tribe*)	Huslia	Shageluk
Canyon Village	Kaltag	Stevens Village
Chalkyitsik	Koyukuk	Takotna
Circle	Lake Minchumina	Tanacross
Dot Lake	(*Minchumina*)	Tanana
Eagle	Manley Hot Springs	Telida
Evansville	McGrath	Tetlin
Fort Yukon	Minto	Venetie

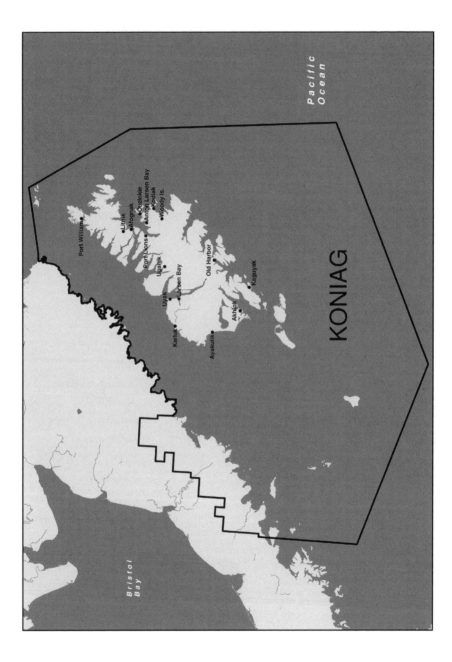

Koniag, Inc.

104 Center Avenue, Suite 205
Kodiak, AK 99615
Office (907) 486-2530
Fax (907) 486-3325
Email kchichenoff@koniag.com
www.koniag.com

Mission: our mission is to optimize profits, and to provide dividends and benefits, while preserving our cultural pride.

Koniag Region Villages (*and Traditional Names*)

Afognak (*Ag'waneq*)
Akhiok (*Kasukuak*)
Anton Larsen Bay
Ayakulik
Bells Flats
Kaguyak
Karluk (*Kal'ut*)
Larsen Bay (*Uyaqsaq*)
Litnik
Old Harbor (*Nuniaq*)
Ouzinkie (*Uusenkaaq*)
Port Lions (*Masiqsiraq*)
Port William
Kodiak (*Sun'aq*)
Uganik
Uyak
Woody Island

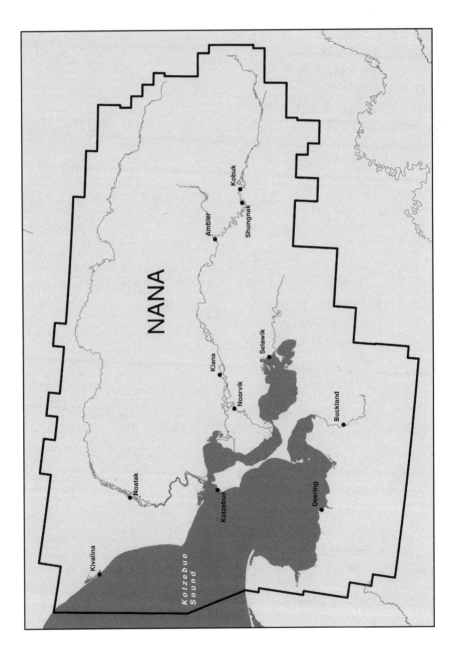

NANA Regional Corporation, Inc.

P.O. Box 49
Kotzebue, AK 99752
Office (907) 442-3301
Fax (907) 442-2866
Email info@nana.com
www.nana.com

Mission: we improve the quality of life for our people by maximizing economic growth, protecting and enhancing our lands, and promoting healthy communities with decisions, actions, and behaviors inspired by Inupiat Ilitqusiat Values, and consistent with our Core Principles.

NANA Region Villages (*and Traditional Names*)

Ambler (*Ivissaappaat*)
Buckland (*Nunatchiaq*)
Deering (*Ipnatchiaq*)
Kiana (*Katvvak*)
Kivalina (*Kivaliniq*)
Kobuk (*Laugviik*)
Kotzebue
Noatak (*Nautaaq*)
Noorvik (*Nuurvik*)
Selawik (*Akuligaq*)
Shungnak (*Isinnaq*)

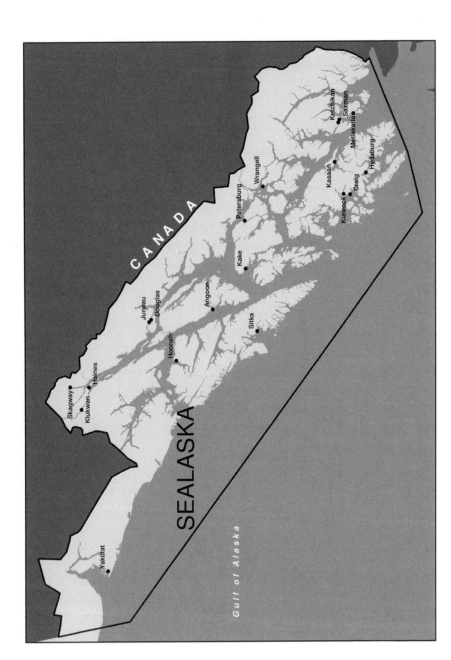

Sealaska Corporation

One Sealaska Plaza #400
Juneau, AK 99801
Office (907) 586-1512
Fax (907) 586-2304
(800) 848-5921
Email CorpSec@sealaska.com
www.sealaska.com

Mission: Sealaska's philosophy is to protect and grow our corporate assets to provide economic, cultural, and social benefits to current and future generations of our shareholders.

Sealaska Region Villages (*and Traditional Names*)

Angoon	Klawock (*Klawak*)
Craig	Klukwan (*Chilkat*)
Douglas	Annette Island Reserve
Haines	(*Metlakatla*)
Hoonah	Petersburg
Hydaburg	Saxman
Juneau	Sitka
Kake	Skagway
Kasaan	Wrangell
Ketchikan	Yakutat

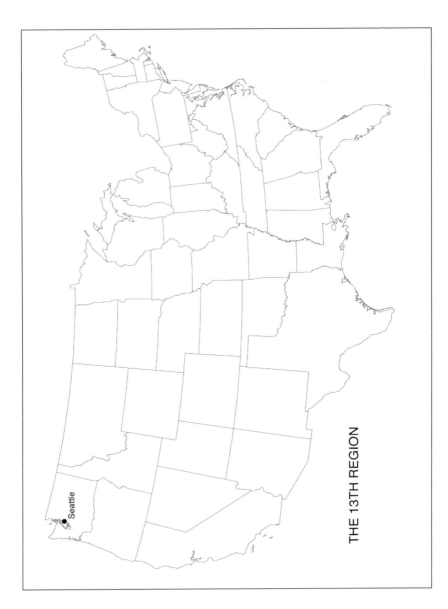

Seattle

THE 13TH REGION

The 13th Regional Corporation

1156 Industry Drive
Tukwila, WA 98188
Office (206) 575-6229x104
Fax (206) 575-6283
Email info@the13thregion.com
www.the13thregion.com

Mission: to allocate resources for our subsidiaries to flourish and oversee investments for the benefit of our shareholders.

VILLAGE CORPORATIONS
LISTED BY REGION

AHTNA ————————————

** No Cantwell Corp.

** No Chistochina Corp

Chitina Native Corporation
P.O. Box 3
Chitina, AK 99566
Office (907) 823–2223
Fax (907) 823–2202
Email chitina@chitinanative.com
chitinanative.com

** No Copper Center Corp.

** No Gakona Corp.

** No Gulkana Corp.

** No Mentasta Lake Corp.

** No Tazlina Corp.

ALEUT ————————————

Akutan Corporation
P.O. Box 8
Akutan, AK 99553
Office (907) 698–2206
Fax (907) 698–2207
Email akutancorporation@hotmail.com

Atxam Corporation
P.O. Box 47001
Atka, AK 99547
Office (907) 839–2237
Fax (907) 839–2217

Belkofski Corporation
P.O. Box 46
King Cove, AK 99612

(False Pass) Isanotski Corporation
P.O. Box 9
False Pass, AK 99583
Office (907) 548–2217
Fax (907) 548–2317
Email isanotskicorp@gci.net
www.isanotski.alaska.com

King Cove Corporation
P.O. Box 38
King Cove, AK 99612
Office (907) 497–2312
Fax (907) 497–2444
Email kcc@arctic.net
www.kingcovecorporation.com

Nelson Lagoon Corporation
P.O. Box 13
Nelson Lagoon, AK 99571
Office (907) 989–2204
Fax (907) 989–2233

(Nikolski) Chaluka Corporation
P.O. Box 104
Nikolski, AK 99638
Office (907) 576–2216
Email chaluka_1@yahoo.com

St. George Tanaq Corporation
4141 B Street, Suite 301
Anchorage, AK 99503
Office (907) 272–9886
Fax (907) 272–9855
Email kkash@stgeorgetanaq.com
www.stgeorgetanaq.com

(St. Paul) Tanadgusix TDX Corporation
4300 B Street, Suite 402
Anchorage, AK 99503
Office (907) 278–2312
Fax (907) 278–2316
Email info@tanadgusix.com
www.tanadgusix.com

Sanak Corporation
P.O. Box 194
Sand Point, AK 99661
Office (907) 383–2601
Fax (907) 383–2601

(Sand Point) Shumagin Corporation
P.O. Box 189
Sand Point, AK 99661
Office (907) 383–3525
Fax (907) 383–5356
www.shumagin.com

Ounalashka Corporation
P.O. Box 149
Unalaska, AK 99685
Office (907) 581–1276
Fax (907) 581–1496
www.ounalashka.com

Unga Corporation
P.O. Box 130
Sand Point, AK 99661
Office (907) 383–5215
Fax (907) 383–5553
Email ungacorp@arctic.net

ARCTIC SLOPE ─────────────

Nunamiut Corporation
P.O. Box 21009
Anaktuvuk Pass, AK 99721
Office (907) 661–3026
Fax (907) 661–3025
Email nunamiutcorp@gci.net

Atqasuk Corporation
Tikilk & Akpik Street
Atqasuk, AK 99791
Office (907) 633–6414
Fax (907) 633–6213
Email atqasukcor@aol.com

(Barrow) Ukpeagvik Inupiat Corporation
P.O. Box 890
Barrow, AK 99723
Office (907) 852–4460
Fax (907) 852–4459
Email Lkanayurak@ukpik.com;
madams@ukpik.com
www.ukpik.com

Kaktovik Inupiat Corporation
P.O. Box 73
Kaktovik, AK 99747
Office (907) 640–6120
Fax (907) 640–6217

(Nuiqsut) Kuukpik Corporation
P.O. Box 89187
Nuiqsut, AK 99789
Office (907) 480–6220
Fax (907) 480–6126
Email INukapigak@kuukpik.com
www.kuukpik.com.

(Point Hope) Tikigaq Corporation
2121 Abbott Road
Anchorage, AK 99507
Office (907) 365–6299
Fax (907) 365–6250
Email jw.graves@tikigaq.com
www.tikigaq.com

(Point Lay) Cully Corporation
Incorporated
405 E Fireweed Lane, Suite 203
Anchorage, AK 99503
Office (907) 569–2705
Fax (907) 569–2715
Email kali@astacalaska.net

Olgoonik Corporation
P.O. Box 29/518 Main Street
Wainwright, AK 99782
Office (907) 763–2613
Fax (907) 763–2926
Email ocinfo@olgoonik.com
www.olgoonik.com

BERING STRAITS ─────────────

Brevig Mission Native Corporation
P.O. Box 24
Brevig Mission, AK 99785
Office (907) 642–4091
Fax (907) 642–2060

Council Native Corporation
P.O. Box 1183
Nome, AK 99762
Office (907) 443–6513

(Diomede) Inalik Native Corporation
P.O. Box 7040
Diomede, AK 99762
Office (907) 686–3221
Fax (907) 686–3222

Elim Native Corporation
P.O. Box 39010
Elim, AK 99739
Office (907) 890–3741
Fax (907) 890–3091
Email elimnativecorp@gci.net

(Gambell) Sivuqaq Incorporated
P.O. Box 101
Gambell, AK 99742
Office (907) 985–5826
Fax (907) 985–5426
Email sivuqaq@gci.net

Golovin Native Corporation
P.O. Box 62099
Golovin, AK 99762
Office (907) 779–3251
Fax (907) 779–3261
Email gnclandplanner@gci.net

King Island Native Corporation
P.O. Box 992
Nome, AK 99762
Office (907) 443–5494
Fax (907) 443–5400
Email kingisland@gci.net

Koyuk Native Corporation
P.O. Box 53050
Koyuk, AK 99753
Office (907) 963–2424
Fax (907) 963–3552
Email koyuknativecorporation@gci.net

Mary's Igloo Native Corporation
P.O. Box 650
Teller, AK 99778
Office (907) 642–2308
Fax (907) 642– 2309

Sitnasuak Native Corporation
P.O. Box 905
Nome, AK 99762
Office (907) 443–2632
Fax (907) 443–3063
www.snc.org

St. Michael Native Corporation
P.O. Box 59049
St. Michael, AK 99659
Office (907) 923–3143
Fax (907) 923–3142
Email saintmichaelnativecorp@gci.net

Savoonga Native Corporation
101 West Benson Blvd. Suite 304
Anchorage, AK 99769

Shaktoolik Native Corporation
P.O. Box 46
Shaktoolik, AK 99771
Office (907) 955–3241
Fax (907) 955–3243
Email fnsago@yahoo.com

Shishmaref Native Corporation
P.O. Box 72151
Shishmaref, AK 99772
Office (907) 649–3751
Fax (907) 649–3731

Solomon Native Corporation
P.O. Box 243
Nome, AK 99762
Office (907) 443–7526
Fax (907) 443–7527

Stebbins Native Corporation
P.O. Box 71110
Stebbins, AK 99671
Office (907) 934–3074
Fax (907) 934–2399

Teller Native Corporation
P.O. Box 590
Teller, AK 99778

Unalakleet Native Corporation
P.O. Box 100
Unalakleet, AK 99684
Office (907) 624–3411
Fax (907) 624–3833
Email uncoffice@ak.net

Wales Native Corporation
P.O. Box 529
Wales, AK 99783–0529
Office (907) 664–3641
Fax (907) 664–3641
Email tcrisci_wnc@yahoo.com

White Mountain Native Corporation
P.O. Box 89
White Mountain, AK 99784
Office (907) 638–2082 or 929–1547
Fax (907) 638–3961

BRISTOL BAY

Aleknagik Natives Limited
P.O. Box 1630
Dillingham, AK 99576–1630
Office (907) 842–2385
Fax (907) 842–1662

(Chignik) Far West, Incorporated
P.O. Box 124
Homer, AK 99603
Office (907) 235–7981
Fax (907) 235–7981

** No Chignik Bay Native Corp.

Chignik Lagoon Native Corporation
P.O. Box 170
Chignik Lagoon, AK 99565
Office (907) 840–2225
Fax (907) 840–2270

Chignik River Limited
P.O. Box 48007
Chignik Lake, AK 99548
Office (907) 845–2261
Fax (907) 845–2262

Saguyak, Incorporated
General Delivery
Clark's Point, AK 99569
Office (907) 236–1235
Fax (907) 236–1450

(Dillingham) Choggiung, Limited
P.O. Box 330
Dillingham, AK 99576
Office (907) 842–5218
Fax (907) 842–5462
bristol–inn.com/choggiung_ltd.htm

(Egegik) Becharof Corporation
1225 E. International Airport Road, Suite 135
Anchorage, AK 99518
Office (907) 561–4777
Fax (907) 561–4778
Email becharof@gci.net

(Ekuk) Choggiung, Limited
P.O. Box 330
Dillingham, AK 99576
Office (907) 842–5218
Fax (907) 842–5462
bristol–inn.com/choggiung_ltd.htm

Ekwok Natives Limited
P.O. Box 1189
Dillingham, AK 99576
Office (907) 842–2385
Fax (907) 842–1662
Email luki2akelkok@yahoo.com

** No Kanatak Native Corp.

** No King Salmon Native Corp.

(Kokhanok) Alaska Peninsula Corporation
111 W. 16th Avenue, Suite 101
Anchorage, AK 99501–6206
Office (907) 274–2433
Fax (907) 274–8694
Email akpc@alaska.net
www.alaskapeninsulacorporation.com

Koliganek Natives Limited
P. O. Box 5057
Koliganek, AK 99576
Office (907) 596–3434
Fax (907) 596–3462

Igiugig Native Corporation
P.O. Box 4009
Igiugig, AK 99613
Office (907) 533–8001
Fax (907) 533–3217
Email igiugig@bristolbay.com
www.igiugig.com

Iliamna Natives Limited
P.O. Box 245
Iliamna, AK 99606
Office (907) 571–1597
Fax (907) 571–1527
Email trefsue@starband.net

Bay View Incorporated
P.O. Box 233407
Anchorage, AK 99523–3407
Office (907) 344–8252
Fax (907) 344–8252
Email shanclan7@yahoo.com

Levelock Natives Limited
P.O. Box 109
Levelock, AK 99625
Office (907) 287–3006
Email levelock@starband.net

Manokotak Natives Limited
P.O. Box 149
Manokotak, AK 99628–0149
Office (907) 289–1062
Fax (907) 289–1007

Paug-Vik Incorporated, Limited
P.O. Box 61
Naknek, AK 99633
Office (907) 246–4277
Fax (907) 246–4419
Email secretary@pvil.com
www.pvil.com

(Newhalen) Alaska Peninsula Corporation
111 W. 16th Avenue, Suite 101
Anchorage, AK 99501
Office (907) 274–2433
Fax (907) 274–8694
Email akpc@alaska.net
www.alaskapeninsulacorporation.com

Stuyahok Limited
P.O. Box 50
New Stuyahok, AK 99636
Office (907) 693–3122
Fax (907) 693–3148

Kijik Corporation
4155 Tudor Centre Drive #104
Anchorage, AK 99508
Office (907) 561–4487
Fax (907) 562–4945

Pedro Bay Native Corporation
P.O. Box 47015
Pedro Bay, AK 99647–0015
Office (907) 850–2323
Fax (907) 850–2221

Oceanside Native Corporation
P.O. Box 84
Perryville, AK 99648
Office (907) 853–2300
Fax (907) 853–2301

Pilot Point Native Corporation
P.O. Box 487
Pilot Point, AK 99649

(Port Alsworth) Tanalian Incorporated
2425 Merrill Field Drive
Anchorage, AK 99501
Office (907) 272–3581
Fax (907) 272–3592

(Port Heiden) Alaska Peninsula
Corporation
111 W. 16th Avenue Suite 101
Anchorage, AK 99501
Office (907) 274–2433
Fax (907) 274–8694
Email akpc@alaska.net
www.alaskapeninsulacorporation.com

(Portage Creek) Choggiung Limited
P.O. Box 330
Dillingham, AK 99576
Office (907) 842–5218
Fax (907) 842–5462
www.bristol-inn.com/choggiung_ltd.htm

(South Naknek) Alaska Peninsula
Corporation
111 West 16th Avenue Suite 101
Anchorage, AK 99501–5109
Office (907) 274–2433
Fax (907) 274–8694
Email akpc@alaska.net
www.alaskapeninsulacorporation.com

Togiak Natives Limited
P.O. Box 150
Togiak, AK 99678
Office (907) 493–5520
Fax (907) 493–5554

Twin Hills Native Corporation
P.O. Box TWA
Twin Hills, AK 99576–8996
Office (907) 525–4327
Fax (907) 525–4820
cybereskimo@starband.net

(Ugashik) Alaska Peninsula Corporation
111 West 16th Avenue, Suite 101
Anchorage, AK 99501–5109
Office (907) 274–2433
Fax (907) 274–8694
Email akpc@alaska.net
www.alaskapeninsulaCorporation.com

CALISTA

Akiachak, Limited
P.O. Box 51010
Akiachak, AK 99551
Office (907) 825–4328
Fax (907) 825–4115
Email akiachakltd@hotmail.com

Kokarmuit Corporation
P.O. Box 52147
Akiak, AK 99552
Office (907) 765–7228
Fax (907) 765–7619

Alakanuk Native Corporation
P.O. Box 148
Alakanuk, AK 99554
Office (907) 238–3117
Fax (907) 238–3120

(Andreafski) Nerkilikmute Native
Corporation
P.O. Box 87
St. Mary's, AK 99658
Office (907) 438–2332
Fax (907) 438–2919
Email nnc@gci.net

(Aniak) The Kuskokwim Corporation
4300 B Street, Suite 207
Anchorage, AK 99503
Office (907) 243–2944
Fax (907) 243–2984
(800) 478–2171
Email blm@kuskokwim.com
www.kuskokwim.com

Atmautluak Limited
P.O. Box 6548
Atmautluak, AK 99559
Office (907) 553–5428
Fax (907) 553–5420

Bethel Native Corporation
P.O. Box 719
Bethel, AK 99559
Office (907) 543–2124
Fax (907) 543–2897
Email ahoffman@bnc-alaska.com
www.bnc-alaska.com

Kongnikilmuit Yuita Corporation
P.O. Box 20308
Kotlik, AK 99620
Office (907) 899–4016
Fax (907) 899–4017

Chefarnrmute Incorporated
P.O. Box 70
Chefornak, AK 99561
Office (907) 867–8115
Fax (907) 867–8895
Email info@chefarnrmuteinc.com
www.chefarnrmuteinc.com

Chevak Company Corporation
P.O. Box 276
Chevak, AK 99563
Office (907) 858–7920
Fax (907) 858–7311
Email chevakcc@unicom-alaska.com

(Chuathbaluk)The Kuskokwim
Corporation
4300 B Street, Suite 207
Anchorage, AK 99503
Office (907) 243–2944
Fax: (907) 243–2984
(800) 478–2171
Email blm@kuskokwim.com
www.kuskokwim.com

Chuloonawick Corporation
2635 Draper Dr
Anchorage, AK 99508

(Crooked Creek) The Kuskokwim
Corporation
4300 B Street, Suite 207
Anchorage, AK 99503
Office (907) 243–2944
Fax (907) 243–2984
(800) 478–2171
Email blm@kuskokwim.com
www.kuskokwim.com

Iqfijouaq Company, Incorporated
P.O. Box 49
Eek, AK 99578
Office (907) 536–5211
Fax (907) 536–5733

Emmonak Corporation
P. O. Box 49
Emmonak, AK 99581
Office (907) 949–1411
Fax (907) 949–1412

(Georgetown) The Kuskokwim
Corporation
4300 B Street, Suite 207
Anchorage, AK 99503
Ofice (907) 243–2944
Fax: (907) 243–2984
(800) 478–2171
Email blm@kuskokwim.com
www.kuskokwim.com

Kuitsarak, Incorporated
P.O. Box 150
Goodnews Bay, AK 99589
Office (907) 967–8428
Fax (907) 967–8226

Nunapiglluraq Corporation
P.O. Box 20187
Kotlik, AK 99620
Office (907) 899–4453
Fax (907) 899–4202

Sea Lion Corporation
P.O. Box 87
Hooper Bay, AK 99604
Office (907) 758–4015
Fax (907) 758–4815
Email sealion@unicom-alaska.com
www.unicom-alaska.com/~slchotel/
index.html

(Upper Kalskag) The Kuskokwim
Corporation
4300 B Street, Suite 207
Anchorage, AK 99503
Office (907) 243–2944
Fax (907) 243–2984
(800) 478–2171
Email blm@kuskokwim.com
www.kuskokwim.com

(Lower Kalskag) The Kuskokwim
Corporation
4300 B Street, Suite 207
Anchorage, AK 99503
Office (907) 243–2944
Fax (907) 243–2984
(800) 478–2171
Email blm@kuskokwim.com
www.kuskokwim.com

Kasigluk Incorporated
P.O. Box 39
Kasigluk, AK 99609
Office (907) 477–6113
Fax (907) 477–6026

(Kipnuk) Kugkaktlik Limited
P.O. Box 36
Kipnuk, AK 99614
Office (907) 896–5414
Fax (907) 896–5140

(Kongiganak) Qemirtalek Coast
Corporation
P.O. Box 5070
Kongiganak, AK 99559
Office (907) 557–5529
Fax (907) 557–5711

Kotlik Yupik Corporation
P.O. Box 20207
Kotlik, AK 99620
Office (907) 899–4014
Fax (907) 899–4528
www.kotlikalaska.com

Kwethluk Incorporated
P.O. Box 110
Kwethluk, AK 99621
Office (907) 757–6613
Fax (907) 757–6212

(Kwigillingok) Kwik Incorporated
P.O. Box 50
Kwigillingok, AK 99622
Office (907) 588–8112
Fax (907) 588–8313

Lime Village Company
P.O. Box LVD
McGrath, AK 99627

Maserculiq Incorporated
P.O. Box 90
Marshall, AK 99585
Office (907) 679–6512
Fax (907) 679–6740
Email maserculiq_incorporated@
yahoo.com

NIMA Corporation
236 West 10th Avenue, Suite 100
Anchorage, AK 99501
Office (907) 563–1566
Fax (907) 568–1567
Email ntoots@nimacorporation.com
www.nimacorporation.com

Azachorok Incorporated
P.O. Box 32213
Mountain Village, AK 99632
Office (907) 591–2527
Fax (907) 591–2127

(Napaimute) The Kuskokwim
Corporation
4300 B Street, Suite 207
Anchorage, AK 99503
Office (907) 243–2944
Fax (907) 243–2984
(800) 478–2171
Email blm@kuskokwim.com
www.kuskokwim.com

Napakiak Corporation
P.O. Box 34030
Napakiak, AK 99634
Office (907) 589–2227
Fax (907) 589–2412

Napaskiak, Incorporated
P.O. Box 6069
Napaskiak, AK 99559
Office (907) 737–7413
Fax (907)737–7128

Newtok Corporation
P.O. Box 5528
Newtok, AK 99559
Office (907) 237–2200
Fax (907) 237–2227

(Nightmute) Chinuruk, Incorporated
P.O. Box 90009
Nightmute, AK 99690
Office (907) 647–6813
Fax (907) 647–6814

Nunapitchuk, Limited
P.O. Box 129
Bethel, AK 99641–0129
Office (907) 527–5717
Fax (907) 527–5229

Ohog Incorporated
P.O. Box 28
Lower Kalskag, AK 99585

Oscarville Native Corporation
P.O. Box 6085
Napaskiak, AK 99559–6085
Office (907) 737–7259

Paimiut Corporation
P.O. Box 240084
Anchorage, AK 99508
Office (907) 561–9878
Fax (907) 563–5398
Email piamiut@alaska.net;
piamiuttraditional@gci.net

Pilot Station Incorporated
P.O. Box 5059
Pilot Station, AK 99650
Office (907) 549–3512
Fax (907) 549–3234

Pitka's Point Native Corporation
P.O. Box 289
St. Mary's, AK 99658
Office (907) 438–2953
Fax (907) 438–2276
Email pitkaspointnc@yahoo.com

Arviq, Incorporated
P.O. Box 9
Platinum, AK 99651
Office (907) 979–8113
Fax (907) 979–8229

Qanirtuuq, Incorporated
P.O. Box 69
Quinhagak, AK 99655
Office (907) 556–8289
Fax (907) 556–8814

(Red Devil) The Kuskokwim Corporation
4300 B Street, Suite 207
Anchorage, AK 99503
Office (907) 243–2944
Fax: (907) 243–2984
(800) 478–2171
Email blm@kuskokwim.com
www.kuskokwim.com

Russian Mission Native Corporation
P.O. Box 48
Russian Mission, AK 99657
Office (907) 584–5885
Fax (907) 584–5311

Saint Mary's Native Corporation
P.O. Box 149
St. Mary's, AK 99658
Office (907) 438–2315
Fax (907) 438–2961

Scammon Bay Association Incorporated
P.O. Box 50
Scammon Bay, AK 99662
Office (907) 558–5211
Fax (907) 558–5963

(Nunam Iqua) Swan Lake Corporation
P.O. Box 25
Nunam Iqua, AK 99666
Office (907) 498–4227
Fax (907) 498–4242

(Sleetmute) The Kuskokwim Corporation
4300 B Street, Suite 207
Anchorage, AK 99503
Office (907) 243–2944
Fax (907) 243–2984
(800) 478–2171
Email blm@kuskokwim.com
www.kuskokwim.com

(Stony River) The Kuskokwim
Corporation
4300 B Street, Suite 207
Anchorage, AK 99503
Office (907) 243–2944
Fax: (907) 243–2984
(800) 478–2171
Email blm@kuskokwim.com
www.kuskokwim.com

(Toksook Bay) Nunakauiak Yupik
Corporation
P.O. Box 37068
Toksook Bay, AK 99637
Office (907) 427–7928
Fax (907) 427–7326

Tulkisarmute, Incorporated
P.O. Box 65
Tuluksak, AK 99679
Office (907) 695–6426

Tununrmiut Rinit Corporation
P.O. Box 89
Tununak, AK 99681
Office (907) 652–6311
Fax (907) 652–6315

Qinarmiut Corporation
P.O. Box 8106
Tuntutuliak, AK 99680
Office (907) 256–2315
Fax (907) 256–2441

(Umkumiut) Chinuruk, Incorporated
P.O. Box 90009
Nightmute, AK 99690
Office (907) 647–6813
Fax (907) 647–6814

CHUGACH

Chenega Corporation
3000 C St, Suite 301
Anchorage, AK 99503
Office (907) 277–5706
Fax (907) 277–5700
www.chenega.com

Eyak Corporation
5700 Old Seward Hwy. Suite 206
Anchorage, AK 99518
Office (907) 334–6971
Fax (907) 334–6973
www.eyakcorporation.com

English Bay General Store
P.O.Box 8012
Nanwalek, AK 99603
Office (907) 281–2208
Fax (907) 281–2220

Port Graham Corporation
P.O. Box 5569
Port Graham, AK 99603–5569
Office (907) 284–2212
Fax (907) 284–2219

Tatitlek Corporation
3003 Minnesota Drive Suite 204
Anchorage, AK 99503
Office (907) 278–4000
Fax (907) 278–4050
Email rtotemoff@tatitlek.com

COOK INLET

Alexander Creek, Incorporated
8128 Cranberry
Anchorage, AK 99502
Office (907) 243–5428
Fax (907) 243–5428

Chickaloon Moose Creek Native
Association, Incorporated
P.O. Box 875046
Wasilla, AK 99687
Office (907) 373–1145
Fax (907) 373–1004
Email cmcnapres@yahoo.com

Eklutna, Incorporated
16515 Centerfield Drive, Suite 201
Eagle River, AK 99577
Office (907) 696–2828
Fax (907) 696–2845
www.eklutnainc.com

(Urban Corp) Kenai Native Association,
Incorporated
215 Fidalgo Avenue #101
Kenai, AK 99611–7776
Office (907) 283–4851
Fax (907) 283–4854

Knikatnu, Incorporated
P.O. Box 872130
Wasilla, AK 99687
Office (907) 376–2845
Fax (907) 376–2847
Email knikcorp@gci.net

Ninilchik Native Association,
Incorporated
701 W. 41st Avenue, Suite 201
Anchorage 99503
Office (907) 567–3866
Fax (907) 344–8634
(888) 301–1058
www.nnai.net

Salamatof Native Association,
Incorporated
P.O. Box 2682
Kenai, AK 99611–2682
Office (907) 283–3745/7864
Fax (907) 283–6470
www.salamatof.net

Seldovia Native Association, Incorporated
P.O. Box L
Seldovia, AK 99663
Office (907) 234–7625
Fax (907) 234–7637
Email snai@snai.com
www.snai.com

Tyonek Native Corporation
1689 C Street, Suite 219
Anchorage, AK 99501–5131
Office (907) 272–0707
Fax (907) 274–7125
(877) 862–6667
Email bperatrovich@tyonek.com
www.tyonek.com

DOYON

(Alatna) K'oyitl'ots'ina, Limited
1603 College Road
Fairbanks, AK 99709
Office (907) 452–8119
Fax (907) 452–8148
(800) 452–8112
www.koyitlotsina.com

(Allakaket) K'oyitl'ots'ina, Limited
1603 Collage Road
Fairbanks, AK 99709
Office (907) 452–8119
Fax (907) 452–8148
(800) 452–8112
www.koyitlotsina.com

(Anvik) Deloy Ges Incorporated
P.O. Box 150
Anvik, AK 99558
Office (907) 663–6396
Fax (907) 663–6355

** No Arctic Village Native Corp.

Beaver Kwit'chin Corporation
P.O. Box 24029
Beaver, AK 99724

(Birch Creek) Tiheet' Aii, Incorporated
P.O. Box KBC
Fort Yukon, AK 99740

(Canyon Village) Kian Tr'ee Corporation
P.O. Box 206
Fort Yukon, AK 99740
Office (907) 662–3442

Chalkyitsik Native Corporation
P.O. Box 53
Chalkyitsik, AK 99788
Office (907) 848–8112
Fax (907) 848–8114

(Circle) Danzhit Hanlaii Corporation
330 Wendell Street, Suite E
Fairbanks, AK 99733

Dot Lake Native Corporation
P.O. Box 2271
Dot Lake, AK 99737
Office (907) 882–2697
Fax (907) 882–2775

(Eagle) Hungwitchin Corporation
P.O. Box 10682
Fairbanks, AK 99710

Evansville, Incorporated
P.O. Box 60670
Fairbanks, AK 99706–0670
Office (907) 374–7084
Fax (907) 374–7085
Email evansvilleinc@hotmail.com

(Fort Yukon) Gwitchyaa Zhee
Corporation
P.O. Box 329
Fort Yukon, AK 99740
Office (907) 662–2933
Fax (907) 662–3056

(Galena) Gana-A' Yoo, Limited
6927 Old Seward Hwy, Suite 101
Anchorage, AK 99518
Office (907) 569–9599
Fax (907) 569–9699
Email bhuntington@ganaayoo.com
www.khotol.com

(Grayling) Hee-Yea-Lingde Corporation
P.O. Box 9
Grayling, AK 99590
Office (907) 453–5133
Fax (907) 453–5151

(Healy Lake) Mendas
Cha-ag Native Corporation
457 Cindy Drive
Fairbanks, AK 99701

(Holy Cross) Deloycheet, Incorporated
P.O. Box 228
Holy Cross, AK 99602
Office (907) 476–7177
Fax (907) 476–7176
Email info@deloycheet.com
www.deloycheet.com

(Hughes) K'oyitl'ots'ina, Limited
1603 College Road
Fairbanks, AK 99709
Office (907) 452–8119
Fax (907) 452–8148
www.koyitlotsina.com

(Huslia) K'oyitl'ots'ina, Limited
1603 College Road
Fairbanks, AK 99709
Office (907) 452–8119
Fax (907) 452–8148
www.koyitlotsina.com

(Kaltag) Gana-A' Yoo Limited
6927 Old Seward Hwy, Suite 101
Anchorage, AK 99518
Office (907) 569–9599
Fax (907) 569–9699
Email bhuntington@ganaayoo.com
www.ganaayoo.com

(Koyukuk) Gana-A' Yoo Limited
6927 Old Seward Hwy, Suite 101
Anchorage, AK 99518
Office (907) 569–9599
Fax (907) 569–9699
Email bhuntington@ganaayoo.com
www.ganaayoo.com

Lake Minchumina, Incorporated
C/O Robert Thompson
Kaktovik, AK 99747
Office (907) 640–6119
(907) 640–6128

(Manley Hot Springs) Bean Ridge
Corporation
P.O. Box 110
Manly Hot Springs, AK 99708
Office (907) 458–2176
Fax (907) 672–3232
Email dixie.doya@uaf.edu

(McGrath) MTNT Limited
P.O. Box 309
McGrath, AK 99627
Office (907) 524–3391
Fax (907) 524–3062
Email mtnt@mcgrathalaska.com

(Minto) Seth-De-Ya-Ah Corporation
P.O. Box 56
Minto, AK 99758
Office (907) 798–7181
Fax (907) 798–7556

(Nenana) Toghotthele Corporation
P.O. Box 249
Nenana, AK 99760
Office (907) 832–5832
Fax (907) 832–5834

(Nikolai) MTNT Limited
P.O. Box 309
McGrath, AK 99627
Office (907) 524–3391
Fax (907) 524–3062
Email mtnt@mcgrathalaska.com

Northway Natives, Incorporated
P.O. Box 476
Northway, AK 99764
Office (907) 778–2298
Fax (907) 778–2498

(Nulato) Gana-A' Yoo Limited
6927 Old Seward Hwy, Suite 101
Anchorage, AK 99518
Office (907) 569–9599
Fax (907) 569–9699
Email bhuntington@ganaayoo.com
www.ganaayoo.com

(Rampart) Baan O Yeel Kon Corporation
P.O. Box 74558
Fairbanks, AK 99707
Office (907) 456–6259
Fax (907) 456–4486
Email boyk@misquitonet.com

(Ruby) Dineega Corporation
P.O. Box 68028
Ruby, AK 99768
Office (907) 468–4405
Fax (907) 468–4403

(Shageluk) Zho-Tse, Incorporated
P.O. Box 130
Shageluk, AK 99665
Office (907) 473–8262
Fax (907) 473–8217

(Stevens Village) Dinyee Corporation and
River Villages, Incorporated
P.O. Box 71372
Fairbanks, AK 99707
Office (907) 452–7162
Fax (907) 452–5063
Email dinyeecorp@acsalaska.net

(Takotna) MTNT Limited
P.O. Box 309
McGrath, AK 99627
Office (907) 524–3391
Fax (907) 524–3062
Email mtnt@mcgrathalaska.com

Tanacross, Incorporated
P.O. Box 76029
Tanacross, AK 99776
Office (907) 883–4130
Fax (907) 883–4129

(Tanana) Tozitna, Limited
P.O. Box 129
Tanana, AK 99777
Office (907) 366–7255
Fax (907) 366–7122

(Telida) MTNT Limited
P.O. Box 309
McGrath, AK 99627
Office (907)524–3391
Fax (907) 524–3062
Email mtnt@mcgrathalaska.com

Tetlin Native Corporation
P.O. Box TTL
Tetlin, AK 99779

** No Venetie Native Corporation **

KONIAG

Afognak Native Corporation
215 Mission Road, Suite 212
Kodiak, AK 99615
Office (907) 486–6014
Fax (907) 486–2514
(800) 770–6014
www.afognak.com

Akhiok–Kaguyak, Incorporated
1400 W. Benson Blvd., Suite 425
Anchorage, AK 99503
Office (907) 258–0604
Fax (907) 258–0608
Email akisr@alaska.net

Anton Larsen, Incorporated
P.O. Box 1366
Kodiak, AK 99615
Office (907) 486–3493

Ayakulik, Incorporated
3741 Richmond Avenue #5
Anchorage, AK 99515
ayakulik@goplay.com

Bells Flats Natives, Incorporated
1877 East Tudor Road, Apt. E–3
Anchorage, AK 99507

** No Karluk Corp.

** No Larsen Bay Native Corp.

Litnik Incorporated
P.O. Box 1962
Kodiak, AK 99615
Office (907) 486–4833
Fax (907) 486–3391

Old Harbor Native Corporation
P.O. Box 71
Old Harbor, AK 99643
Office (907) 286–2286
Fax (907) 286–2287
Email ohnc@starband.net

Ouzinkie Native Corporation
P.O. Box 89
Ouzinkie, AK 99644
Office (907) 680–2208
Fax (907) 680–2268
Email mdebraonc@starband.net
www.ouzinkienativecorporation.com

(Port Lions) Afognak Native Corporation
215 Mission Road, Suite 212
Kodiak, AK 99615
Office (907) 486–6014
Fax (907) 486–2514
(800) 770–6014
www.afognak.com

(Port William) Shuyak, Incorporated
P.O. Box 727
Kodiak, AK 99615
Office (907) 486–3842
Fax (907) 486–5097

(Urban Corp) Natives of Kodiak,
Incorporated
215 Mission Road #201
Kodiak, AK 99615
Office (907) 486–3606
Fax (907) 486–2745
Email nokinfo@alaska.com
www.nativesofkodiak.com

Uganik Natives, Incorporated
P.O. Box 241963
Anchorage, AK 99524

Uyak, Incorporated
P.O. Box 31
Chignik, AK 99564
Office (928) 453–6637
Fax (928) 453–6637

(Woody Island) Leisnoi, Incorporated
3055–127 North Red Mountain
Mesa, AZ 85207
Office (480) 471–8213 or 907–222–6900
Fax (480) 471–8213
Email cepagano@cox.net

NANA

** No Ambler Corp.

** No Buckland Corp.

** No Deering Corp.

** No Kiana Corp.

** No Kivalina Corp.

** No Kobuk Corp.

(Kotzebue) Kikiktagruk Inupiat
Corporation
P.O. Box 1050
Kotzebue, AK 99752
Office (907) 442–3165
Fax (907) 442–2165
Email info@kiCorporationorg
www.kiCorporationorg

** No Noatak Corp.

** No Noorvik Corp.

** No Selawik Corp.

** No Shungnak Corp.

SEALASKA

(Angoon) Kootznoowoo, Incorporated
8585 Old Dairy Road, Suite 104
Juneau, AK 99801
Office (907) 790–2992
Fax (907) 790–2995
Email peter@kootznoowoo.com
www.kootznoowoo.com

(Craig) Shaan-Seet, Incorporated
P.O. Box 690
Craig, AK 99921
Office (907) 826–3251
Email ssinc@aptalaska.net

** No Douglas Native Corp.

** No Haines Native Corp.

(Hoonah) Huna Totem Corporation
9301 Glacier Hwy., Suite 200
Juneau, AK 99801
Office (907) 523–3670
Fax (907) 789–1896
www.hunatotem.com

(Hydaburg) Haida Corporation
P.O. Box 89
Hydaburg, AK 99922
Office (907) 285–3721
Fax (907) 285–3944
Email geanna_morrison85022@yahoo.com
www.haidacorp.com

(Aukquan Urban Corp) Goldbelt, Incorporated
3075 Vintage Blvd, Suite 200
Juneau, AK 99801
Office (907) 790–4990
Fax (907) 790–4999
Email mail.gbi@goldbelt.com
www.goldbelt.com

Kake Tribal Corporation
P.O. Box 263
Kake, AK 99830
Office (907) 785–3221
Fax (907) 785–6407

(Kasaan) Kavilco, Incorporated
P.O. Box KXA
Ketchikan, AK 99950–0340
Office (907) 542–2214
Fax (907) 542–2215
Email dee_kavilco@msn.com
www.kavilco.com

Klawock Heenya Corporation
P.O. Box 129
Klawock, AK 99925
Office (907) 755–2270
Fax (907) 755–2966
Email khc@aptalaska.net
www.klawockheenya.com

** No Ketchikan Native Corp.

Klukwan, Incorporated
P.O. Box 209
Haines, AK 99827
Office (907) 766–2211
Fax (907) 766–2973
Email info@klukwan.com
www.klukwan.com

** No Metlakatla Native Corp.

** No Petersburg Native Corp.

(Saxman) Cape Fox Corporation
P.O. Box 8558
Ketchikan, AK 99901
Office (907) 225–5163
Fax (907) 225–3137
Email dlauth@capefoxcorporation.com
www.capefoxcorporation.com

(Sitka Urban Corporation) Shee Atika, Incorporated
315 Lincoln Street, Suite 300
Sitka, AK 99835
Office (907) 747–3534
Fax (907) 747–5727
(800) 478–3534
Email info@sheeatika.com
www.sheeatika.com

** No Skagway Native Corp.

** No Wrangell Native Corp.

(Yakutat) Yak-Tat Kwaan, Incorporated
P.O. Box 416
Yakutat, AK 99689
Office (907) 784–3335
Fax (907) 784–3266

TRADITIONAL/IRA COUNCILS
LISTED BY REGION

AHTNA

Native Village of Cantwell
P.O. Box 94
Cantwell, AK 99729
Office (907) 768–2591
Fax (907) 768–1111
Email hallvc@mtaonline.net

Chistochina Tribal Council
P.O. Box 241
Gakona, AK 99586
Office (907) 822–3503
Fax (907) 822–5179
Email sgreen@cheeshna.com
www.mstc.org

Chitina Village Council
P.O. Box 31
Chitina, AK 99566–0031
Office (907) 823–2215
Fax (907) 823–2233
Email admin.ctivc@starband.net

Native Village of
Kluti-Kaah (Copper Center)
P.O. Box 68
Copper Center, AK 99573
Office (907) 822–5541
Email nvkktops@cvinternet.net

Gakona Village Council
P.O. Box 102
Gakona, AK 99586
Office (907) 822–5777
Fax (907) 822–5997
Email gakonavc@cvinternet.net

Gulkana Village Council
P.O. Box 254
Gakona, AK 99586
Office (907) 822–3746
Fax (907) 822–3976
Email admin@gulkanacouncil.org
gulkanacouncil.org

Mentasta Tribal Council
P.O. Box 6019
Mentasta Lake, AK 99780
Office (907) 291–2319
Fax (907) 291–2305
Email SryanS123@yahoo.com
www.mstc.org

Tazlina Village Council
P.O. Box 87
Glennallen, AK 99588
Office (907) 822–4375
Fax (907) 822–5865
Email Tazlina@cvinternet.net

ALEUT

Native Village of Akutan
P.O. Box 89
Akutan, AK 99553–0089
Office (907) 698–2300
Fax (907) 698–2301
Email akutanaleuttribe@gci.net

Atka IRA
P.O. Box 47030
Atka, AK 99547
Office (907) 839–2229
Fax (907) 839–2269
Email atkaira@gci.net

Belkofski Tribal Council
P.O. Box 57
King Cove, AK 99612
Office (907) 497–3122
Fax (907) 497–3123
Email kcbtc@arctic.net

False Pass Tribal Council
P.O. Box 29
False Pass, AK 99583
Office (907) 548–2227
Fax (907) 548–2256

Agdaagux Tribe of King Cove
P.O. Box 249
King Cove, AK 99612
Office (907) 497–2648
Fax (907) 497–2803
Email atc@arctic.net

Native Village of Nelson Lagoon
P.O. Box 13
Nelson Lagoon, AK 99571
Office (907) 989–2204
Fax (907) 989–2233

Native Village of Nikolski
P.O. Box 105
Nikolski, AK 99638
Office (907) 576–2225
Fax (907) 576–2205
Email iko.tribe@hotmail.com or
ikotribeadmin@ak.net

St. George Traditional Council
P.O. Box 940
St. George Island, AK 99591
Office (907) 859–2205
Fax (907) 859–2242
Email stgcouncil@starband.net

Aleut Community of St. Paul Island
P.O. Box 86
St. Paul Island, AK 99660
Office (907) 546–3200
Fax (907) 546–3254

Pauloff Harbor Tribe
P.O. Box 97
Sand Point, AK 99661
Office (907) 383–6075
Fax (907) 383–6094
Email pauloff@arctic.net

Qagan Tayagungin Tribe of Sand Point
P.O. Box 447
Sand Point, AK 99661
Office (907) 383–5616
Fax (907) 383–5814
Email qttadmin@arctic.net

Qawalangin Tribe of Unalaska
P.O. Box 334
Unalaska, AK 99685
Office (907) 581–2920
Fax (907) 581–3644
Email qtuunga@arctic.net
www.qawalangin.org

Unga Tribal Council
P.O. Box 508
Sand Point, AK 99661
Office (907) 383–2415
Fax (907) 383–5553
Email ungacorp@arctic.net

ARCTIC SLOPE

Village of Anaktuvuk Pass
P.O. Box 21065
Anaktuvuk Pass, AK 99721
Office (907) 661–2575
Fax (907) 661–2576
Email icasakp@astacalaska.net

Atqasuk Village
P.O. Box 91108
Atqasuk, AK 99791
Office (907) 633–2575
Fax (907) 633–2576
Email icasatq@astacalaska.net

Native Village of Barrow
P.O. Box 1130
Barrow, AK 99723
Office (907) 852–4411
Fax (907) 852–8844
Email tolemaun@nvbarrow.net

Kaktovik Village
P.O. Box 130
Kaktovik, AK 99747
Office (907) 640–2042
Fax (907) 640–2044
Email nvkaktovik@starband.net

Native Village of Nuiqsut
P.O. Box 89169
Nuiqsut, AK 99789–0169
Office (907) 480–3010
Fax (907) 480–3009
Email tanvn@astacalaska.net

Native Village of Point Hope
P.O. Box 109
Point Hope, AK 99766
Office (907) 368–2330
Fax (907) 368–2332
Email aggie.henry@tikigaq.org

Native Village of Point Lay
P.O. Box 59031
Point Lay, AK 99759
Office (907) 833–2575
Fax (907) 833–2576
Email icaspiz@astacalaska.net

Native Village of Wainwright
P.O. Box 143
Wainwright, AK 99782
Office (907) 763–2535
Fax (907) 763–2536

BERING STRAITS

Brevig Traditional Council
P.O. Box 85039
Brevig Mission, AK 99785
Office (907) 642–4301
Fax (907) 642–2099
Email tc2.kts@kawerak.org
www.kawerak.org/tribalHomePages/
brevig/index.html

Council Traditional Council
P.O. Box 2050
Nome, AK 99762
Office (907) 443–7649
Fax (907) 443–5965
Email council@alaska.com
www.kawerak.org/tribalHomePages/
council/index.html

Native Village of Diomede IRA Council
P.O. Box 7079
Diomede, AK 99762
Office (907) 686–2175
Fax (907) 686–2203
www.kawerak.org/tribalHomePages/
diomede/index.html

Native Village of Elim
P.O. Box 39070
Elim, AK 99739
Office (907) 890–3737
Fax (907) 890–3738
Email eli.tc@kawerak.org
www.kawerak.org/tribalHomePages/elim/
index.html

Native Village of Gambell
P.O. Box 90
Gambell, AK 99742
Office (907) 985–5346
Fax (907) 985–5014
Email btungiyan@yahoo.com
www.kawerak.org/tribalHomePages/
gambell/index.html

(Golovin) Chinik Eskimo Community
P.O. Box 62020
Golovin, AK 99762
Office (907) 779–2214
Fax (907) 779–2829
Email slewis@kawerak.org
www.kawerak.org/tribalHomePages/
golovin/index.html

King Island Native Community
P.O. Box 682
Nome, AK 99762
Office (907) 443–2209
Fax (907) 443–8049
Email tc.kingis@kawerak.org
www.kawerak.org/tribalHomePages/
kingIsland/index.html

Koyuk IRA
P.O. Box 30
Koyuk, AK 99753
Office (907) 963–3651
Fax (907) 963–2353
Email arlene@kawerak.org
www.kawerak.org/tribalHomePages/
koyuk/index.html

Mary's Igloo Traditional Council
P.O. Box 546
Mary's Igloo, AK 99778
Office (907) 642–3731
Fax (907) 642–2189
Email tc.mi@kawerak.org
www.kawerak.org/tribalHomePages/
marysIgloo/index.html

Nome Eskimo Community
P.O. Box 1090
Nome, AK 99762
Office (907) 443–2246
Fax (907) 443–3539
Email nomeeskimo@gci.net
www.kawerak.org/tribalHomePages/
nomeEskimo/index.html

St. Michael IRA
P.O. Box 59050
St. Michael, AK 99659
Office (907) 923–2304
Fax (907) 923–2406
www.kawerak.org/tribalHomePages/
stMichael/index.html

Native Village of Savoonga
P.O. Box 120
Savoonga, AK 99769
Office (907) 984–6414
Fax (907) 984–6027
Email valerien@kawerak.org
www.kawerak.org/tribalHomePages/
savoonga/index.html

Shaktoolik IRA
P.O. Box 100
Shaktoolik, AK 99771
Office (907) 955–3701
Fax (907) 955–2352
Email kshgoonick@kawerak.org
www.kawerak.org/tribalHomePages/
shaktoolik/index.html

Shishmaref IRA
P.O. Box 72110
Shishmaref, AK 99772
Office (907) 649–3821
Fax (907) 649–2104
Email nkokeok@kawerak.org
www.kawerak.org/tribalHomePages/
shishmaref/index.html

Solomon Traditional Council
P.O. Box 2053
Nome, AK 99762
Office (907) 443–4985
Fax (907) 443–5189
Email @kawerak.org
www.kawerak.org/tribalHomePages/
solomon/index.html

Stebbins Community Association
P.O. Box 2
Stebbins, AK 99671
Office (907) 934–3561
Fax (907) 934–3560
Email Stebbins_ira@yahoo.com
www.kawerak.org/tribalHomePages/
Stebbins/index.html

Teller Traditional Council
P.O. Box 567
Teller, AK 99778
Office (907) 642–3381
Fax (907) 642–2072
Email cisabell@kawerak.org
www.kawerak.org/tribalHomePages/
teller/index.html

Native Village of Unalakleet
P.O. Box 270
Unalakleet, AK 99684
Office (907) 624–3622
Fax (907) 624–3621
Email unkira@kawerak.org
www.kawerak.org/tribalHomePages/
unalakleet/index.html

Native Village of Wales
P.O. Box 549
Wales, AK 99783
Office (907) 664–3062
Fax (907) 664–2200
Email tc.waa@kawerak.org
www.kawerak.org/tribalHomePages/
wales/index.html

White Mountain IRA
P.O. Box 90
White Mountain, AK 99784
Office (907) 638–3651
Fax (907) 638–3652
Email tc.wmo@kawerak.org
www.kawerak.org/tribalHomePages/
whiteMountain/index.html

BRISTOL BAY

Native Village of Aleknagik
P.O. Box 115
Aleknagik, AK 99555
Office (907) 842–2080
Fax (907) 842–2081
Email aleknagiktraditional@yahoo.com

Chignik Tribal Council
Same as Chignik Bay Tribal Council

Chignik Bay Tribal Council
P.O. Box 50
Chignik, AK 99564
Office (907) 749–2445
Fax (907) 749–2423
Email cbaytc@aol.com

Native Village of Chignik Lagoon
P.O. Box 09
Chignik Lagoon, AK 99565
Office (907) 840–2281
Fax (907) 840–2217
Email clagoon@gci.net

Chignik Lake Traditional Council
P.O. Box 33
Chignik Lake, AK 99548
Office (907) 845–2212
Fax (907) 845–2217
Email chigniklakecouncil@yahoo.com

Clark's Point Village Council
P.O. Box 90
Clark's Point, AK 99569–0090
Office (907) 236–1435
Fax (907) 236–1428

(Dillingham) Curyung Tribal Council
P.O. Box 216
Dillingham, AK 99576
Office (907) 842–2384
Fax (907) 842–4510
www.bbna.com/crg/curyung/index.htm

Egegik Village Tribal Council
6348 Nielsen Way Unit B
Anchorage, AK 99518
Office (907) 563–0056
Fax (907) 563–0058
Email egegiktribaloffice@yahoo.com

Ekuk Village Council
P.O. Box 530
Dillingham, AK 99576
Office (907) 842–3842
Fax (907) 842–3843
Email ekuktrib@starband.net

Ekwok Village Council
P.O. Box 70
Ekwok, AK 99580
Office (907) 464–3336
Fax (907) 464–3378
Email ekwokvillagecouncil@starband.net

Kanatak Village Council
P.O Box 872231
Wasilla, AK 99687
Office (907) 357–5991
Fax (907) 357–5992
(888) 417–7271
Email Kanatak@mtaonline.net
www.kanatak.com

King Salmon Village Council
P.O. Box 68
King Salmon, AK 99613–0068
Office (907) 246–3553
Fax (907) 246–3449
Email kstvc@starband.net

Kokhanok Village Council
P.O. Box 1007
Kokhanok, AK 99606–1007
Office (907) 282–2202
Fax (907) 282–2264
Email kokhanok_vc@yahoo.com;
kvc_housingdept@msn.com

Koliganek Village Council
P.O. Box 5057
Koliganek, AK 99576–5057
Office (907) 596–3434
Fax (907) 596–3462

Igiugig Village Council
P.O. Box 4008
Igiugig, AK 99613
Office (907) 533–3211
Fax (907) 533–3217
Email igiugig@bristolbay.com
igiugig.freeservers.com

Iliamna Village Council
P.O. Box 286
Iliamna, AK 99606
Office (907) 571–1246
Fax (907) 571–1256
Email ilivc@aol.com
www.arctic.net/~newhalen/IliVillage
Council/IliamnaVillageCouncil.html

Ivanof Bay Village Council
2518 E. Tudor Road
Anchorage, AK 99507
Office (907) 522–2263
Fax (907) 522–2363
Email ibvc@ivanofbay.com

Levelock Village Council
P.O. Box 70
Levelock, AK 99625
Office (907) 287–3030
Fax (907) 287–3032
Email levelock@starband.net

Manokotak Village Council
P.O. Box 169
Manokotak, AK 99628
Office (907) 289–2067
Fax (907) 289–1235
Email mnkvc@bbna.com

Naknek Village Council
P.O. Box 106
Naknek, AK 99633
Office (907) 246–4210
Fax (907) 246–3563
Email nnvcak@bristolbay.com

Newhalen Tribal Council
P.O. Box 207
Newhalen, AK 99606
Office (907) 571–1410
Fax (907) 571–1537
Email newhalentribal@yahoo.com
www.arctic.net/~newhalen/Tribalpage/
TribalCouncil.html

New Stuyahok Traditional Council
P.O. Box 49
New Stuyahok, AK 99636
Office (907) 693–3173
Fax (907) 693–3179
Email nstc@starband.net

Nondalton Tribal Council
P.O. Box 49
Nondalton, AK 99640
Office (907) 294–2220
Fax (907) 294–2234
Email ntcadmin@gci.net

Pedro Bay Village Council
P.O. Box 47020
Pedro Bay, AK 99647
Office (907) 850–2225
Fax (907) 850–2221
Email thecouncil@pedrobay.com
www.pedrobay.com

Native Village of Perryville
P.O. Box 89
Perryville, AK 99648
Office (907) 853–2203
Fax (907) 853–2230
Email nvproads@hotmail.com

Pilot Point Village Council
P.O. Box 449
Pilot Point, AK 99649
Office (907) 797–2208
Fax (907) 797–2258
Email capemenshikof@yahoo.com

** No Port Alsworth Village Council

Native Council of Port Heiden
P.O. Box 49007
Port Heiden, AK 99549
Office (907) 837–2296
Fax (907) 837–2297
Email lcarlson79@hotmail.com

Portage Creek Village Council
1327 E. 72nd Avenue, Unit B
Anchorage, AK 99518–2373
Office (907) 277–1105
Email ciugtaq@yahoo.com

South Naknek Village Council
P.O. Box 70029
South Naknek, AK 99670
Office (907) 246–8614
Fax (907) 246–8613
Email southnaknek@starband.net
www.bbna.com/villages/snaknek/
snaknek1b.htm

Togiak Traditional Council
P.O. Box 310
Togiak, AK 99678–0310
Office (907) 493–5003
Fax (907) 493–5005
Email tradcounciltogiak@starband.net

Twin Hills Village Council
P.O. Box TWA
Twin Hills, AK 99576–8996
Office (907) 525–4821
Fax (907) 525–4822
Email william15@starband.net

Ugashik Traditional Village Council
206 E. Fireweed Lane, Suite 204
Anchorage, AK 99503
Office (907) 338–7611
Fax (907) 338–7659
Email information@ugashik.com
www.ugashik.com

CALISTA

Akiachak Native Community
P.O. Box 51070
Akiachak, AK 99551–1070
Office (907) 825–4626
Fax (907) 825–4029
Email anc_tribalcouncils@yahoo.com

Akiak Native Community
P.O. Box 52127
Akiak, AK 99552
Office (907) 765–7112
Fax (907) 765–7512
Email akiaknc@unicom-alaska.com

Alakanuk Traditional Council
P.O. Box 149
Alakanuk, AK 99554–0149
Office (907) 238–3419
Fax (907) 238–3429
Email auktc@unicom-alaska.com

Yupiit of Andreafski
P.O. Box 88
St. Mary's, AK 99658–0088
Office (907) 438–2312
Fax (907) 438–2512
Email andreafski@hotmail.com

Aniak Traditional Council
P.O. Box 349
Aniak, AK 99557
Office (907) 675–4349
Fax (907) 675–4513
Email aniaktc@yahoo.com

Atmautluak Traditional Council
P.O. Box 6568
Atmautluak, AK 99559
Office (907) 553–5610
Fax (907) 553–5612
Email atmautluaktc@hughes.net

Orutsararmiut Native Council
P.O. Box 927
Bethel, AK 99559–0927
Office (907) 543–2608
Fax (907) 543–2639
Email msamuelson@nativecouncil.org

Native Village of Bill Moore's Slough
P.O. Box 20288
Kotlik, AK 99620
Office (907) 899–4232
Fax (907) 899–4461
Email paulineo@gci.net

Chefornak Traditional Council
P.O. Box 110
Chefornak, AK 99561–0110
Office (907) 867–8850
Fax (907) 867–8711
Email cyf_tcoffice@yahoo.com

Chevak Traditional Council
P.O. Box 140
Chevak, AK 99563
Office (907) 858–7428
Fax (907) 858–7812
Email chevaktc@unicom-alaska.com

Chuathbaluk Traditional Council
P.O. Box CHU
Chuathbaluk, AK 99557–8999
Office (907) 467–4313
Fax (907) 467–4113

Native Village of Chuloonawick
P.O. Box 245
Emmonak, AK 99581–0245
Office (907) 949–1345
Fax (907) 949–1346
Email coffice@unicom-alaska.com

Crooked Creek Traditional Council
P.O. Box 69
Crooked Creek, AK 99575
Office (907) 432–2200
Fax (907) 432–2201
Email bbcc@starband.net

Eek Traditional Council
P.O. Box 89
Eek, AK 99578
Office (907) 536–5128
Fax (907) 536–5711
Email etcgov@yahoo.com

Emmonak Tribal Council
P.O. Box 126
Emmonak, AK 99581
Office (907) 949–1720
Fax (907) 949–1384
Email etcadmin@unicom-alaska.com

Georgetown Tribal Council
4300 B Street, Suite 207
Anchorage, AK 99503
Office (907) 274–2195
Fax (907) 274–2196
(888) 274–2195
Email gtc@gci.net
www.georgetowntc.com

Native Village of Goodnews Bay
P.O. Box 138
Goodnews Bay, AK 99589
Office (907) 967–8929
Fax (907) 967–8330
Email goodnews907@hotmail.com

Hamilton Tribal Council
P.O. Box 20248
Kotlik, AK 99620
Office (907) 899–4252
Fax (907) 899–4202
Email iwilliams@avcp.org

Native Village of Hooper Bay
P.O. Box 69
Hooper Bay, AK 99604
Office (907) 758–4915
Fax (907) 758–4066
Email cucipuk@yahoo.com; smartea04@
yahoo.com

Native Village of Upper Kalskag
P.O. Box 50
Kalskag, AK 99607
Office (907) 471–2207
Fax (907) 471–2399
Email bonniealoysius@yahoo.com

Village of Lower Kalskag
P.O. Box 27
Lower Kalskag, AK 99626
Office (907) 471–2379
Fax (907) 471–2378

Kasigluk Traditional Council
P.O. Box 19
Kasigluk, AK 99609
Office (907) 477–6405
Fax (907) 477–6212
Email kukvc@unicom-alaska.com

Kipnuk Traditional Council
P.O. Box 57
Kipnuk, AK 99614
Office (907) 896–5515
Fax (907) 896–5240
Email kipnuktraditional@starband.net

Kongiganak Traditional Council
P.O. Box 5069
Kongiganak, AK 99545–5069
Office (907) 557–5226
Fax (907) 557–5224
Email oactive@avcp.org

Kotlik Traditional Council
P.O. Box 20210
Kotlik, AK 99620
Office (907) 899–4326
Fax (907) 899–4790
Email kotlikpc@yahoo.com

Organized Village of Kwethluk
P.O. Box 130
Kwethluk, AK 99621
Office (907) 757–6714
Fax (907) 757–6328
Email kwtira@unicom-alaska.com

Kwigillingok IRA Council
P.O. Box 49
Kwigillingok, AK 99622–0049
Office (907) 588–8114
Fax (907) 588–8429
Email kwkadmin@starband.net

Lime Village Traditional Council
P. O. Box LVD
McGrath, AK 99627
Office (907) 526–5236
Fax (907) 526–5235
Email limevillage@gmail.com

Native Village of Marshall
P.O. Box 110
Marshall, AK 99585
Office (907) 679–6302
Fax (907) 679–6187

Native Village of Mekoryuk
P.O. Box 66
Mekoryuk, AK 99630
Office (907) 827–8828
Fax (907) 827–8133
Email mekoryukira@yahoo.com

Asa'Carsarmiut Tribal Council
P.O. Box 32249
Mountain Village, AK 99632
Office (907) 591–2814
Fax (907) 591–2811
Email atcadmin@gci.net

Native Village of Napaimute
P.O. Box 1301
Bethel, AK 99559
Office (907) 543–2887
Fax (907) 543–2892
Email napaimute@avcp.org
www.napaimute.org

Napakiak IRA Council
P.O. Box 34069
Napakiak, AK 99634
Office (907) 589–2135
Fax (907) 589–2136
Email napakiak@unicom-alaska.com

Native Village of Napaskiak
P.O. Box 6009
Napaskiak, AK 99559
Office (907) 737–7364
Fax (907) 737–7039
Email pnicholai@napaskiak.org

Newtok Traditional Council
P.O. Box 5545
Newtok, AK 99559
Office (907) 237–2314
Fax (907) 237–2321
Email ntcamaii@yahoo.com

Nightmute Traditional Council
P.O. Box 90021
Nightmute, AK 99690
Office (907) 647–6215
Fax (907) 647–6112

Native Village of Nunapitchuk
P.O. Box 130
Nunapitchuk, AK 99641
Office (907) 527–5705
Fax (907) 527–5711
Email nunap.admin@gmail.com

Ohogamiut Traditional Council
P.O. Box 49
Marshall, AK 99585
Office (907) 679–6517
Fax (907) 679–6516
Email nandrew@gci.net

Oscarville Traditional Council
P.O. Box 6129
Napaskiak, AK 99559
Office (907) 737–7099
Fax (907) 737–7428
Email mStevens@avcp.org

Paimiut Traditional Council
P.O. Box 230
Hooper Bay, AK 99604
Office (907) 758–4002
Fax (907) 758–4024
Email paimiut@alaska.net

Pilot Station Traditional Council
P.O. Box 5119
Pilot Station, AK 99650
Office (907) 549–3373
Fax (907) 549–3301

Native Village of Pitka's Point
P.O. Box 127
St. Mary's, AK 99658
Office (907) 438–2833
Fax (907) 438–2569
Email pitkaspoint@msn.com

Platinum Traditional Village
P.O. Box 8
Platinum, AK 99651
Office (907) 979–8220
Fax (907) 979–8178
Email ptutribal@hotmail.com

Native Village of Qwinhagak
P.O. Box 149
Quinhagak, AK 99655
Office (907) 556–8165
Fax (907) 556–8166
Email ljohnson.nvk@gmail.com

Red Devil Traditional Council
P.O. Box 61
Red Devil, AK 99656
Office (907) 447–3223
Fax (907) 447–3224

(Russian Mission) Iqurmiut
Traditional Council
P.O. Box 9
Russian Mission, AK 99657
Office (907) 584–5511
Fax (907) 584–5593
Email denise_kozevnikoff@yahoo.com

Algaaciq Native Village
P.O. Box 48
St. Mary's, AK 99658
Office (907) 438–2932
Fax (907) 438–2227
Email algaaciq@yahoo.com

Scammon Bay Traditional Council
P.O. Box 126
Scammon Bay, AK 99662
Office (907) 558–5425
Fax (907) 558–5134
Email scammonbay@starband.net

Native Village of Nunam Iqua
P.O. Box 27
Nunam Iqua, AK 99666
Office (907) 498–4184
Fax (907) 498–4185

Sleetmute Traditional Council
P.O. Box 109
Sleetmute, AK 99668
Office (907) 449–4205
Fax (907) 449–4203
Email sleetmutetraditionalcouncil@
yahoo.com

Stony River Traditional Council
P.O. Box SRV
Stony River, AK 99557
Office (907) 537–3253
Fax (907) 537–3254

(Toksook Bay) Nunakauyak Traditional
Council
P.O. Box 37048
Toksook Bay, AK 99637
Office (907) 427–7114
Fax (907) 427–7114
Email nunakauyaktc@hotmail.com

Tuluksak Native Community
P.O. Box 95
Tuluksak, AK 99679–0095
Office (907) 695–6420
Fax (907) 695–6932
Email tmceigap@yahoo.com;
tuluksak@aitc.org

Tununak IRA Council
P.O. Box 77
Tununak, AK 99681
Office (907) 652–6527
Fax (907) 652–6011
Email tribe2work@yahoo.com

Tuntutuliak Traditional Council
P.O. Box 8086
Tuntutuliak, AK 99680
Office (907) 256–2128
Fax (907) 256–2080
Email renoch@avcp.org

Umkumiut Tribal Council
P.O. Box 90062
Nightmute, AK 99690
Office (907) 647–6145
Fax (907) 647–6146

CHUGACH

Chenega IRA
P.O. Box 8079
Chenega Bay, AK 99574–8079
Office (907) 573–5132
Fax (907) 573–5120
Email chenegaira@yahoo.com
www.chugachmiut.org/tribes/
chenega.html

Native Village of Eyak
P.O. Box 1388
Cordova, AK 99574
Office (907) 424–7738
Fax (907) 424–7739
www.nveyak.com

Nanwalek IRA Council
P.O. Box 8028
Nanwalek, AK 99603–8028
Office (907) 281–2274
Fax (907) 281–2252
Email nanwalek@yahoo.com
www.chugachmiut.org/tribes/
nanwalek.html

Port Graham Village Council
P.O. Box 5510
Port Graham, AK 99603
Office (907) 284–2227
Fax (907) 284–2222
www.chugachmiut.org/tribes/Port_
graham.html

Tatitlek Village Council
P.O. Box 171
Tatitlek, AK 99677
Office (907) 325–2311
www.chugachmiut.org/tribes/tatitlek.html

Qutekcak Native Tribe
P.O. Box 1467
Seward, AK 99664–1467
Office (907) 224–3118
Fax 907–224–5874
Email tribaladmin@qutekcak.net
www.qutekcak.net

COOK INLET ─────────

** No Alexander Creek Village Council

Chickaloon Village Traditional Council
P.O. Box 1105
Chickaloon, AK 99674
Office (907) 745–0707
Fax (907) 745–0709
Email info@chickaloon.org
www.chickaloon.org

Native Village of Eklutna
26339 Eklutna Village Road
Chugiak, AK 99567
Office (907) 688–6020
Fax (907) 688–6021
Email nve@eklutna-nsn.gov
www.eklutna-nsn.gov

Kenaitze Indian Tribe
P.O. Box 988
Kenai, AK 99611–0988
Office (907) 283–3633
Fax (907) 283–3052
www.kenaitze.org

Knik Tribal Council
P.O. Box 871565
Wasilla, AK 99687
Office (907) 373–7991
Fax (907) 373–2161
Email kniktrib@mtaonline.net

Ninilchik Traditional Council
P.O. Box 39070
Ninilchik, AK 99639
Office (907) 567–3313
Fax (907) 567–3308
Email ntc@ninilchiktribe-nsn.gov
www.ninilchiktribe-nsn.gov

Village of Salamatof
P.O. Box 2682
Kenai, AK 99611
Office (907) 283–7864
Fax (907) 283–6470
Email snainc@alaska.com

Seldovia Village Tribe
Drawer L
Seldovia, AK 99663
Office (907) 234–7898
Fax (907) 234–7865
Email tgallien@svt.org
www.svt.org

Native Village of Tyonek
P.O. Box 82009
Tyonek, AK 99682–0009
Office (907) 583–2201
Fax (907) 583–2442
Email janelle_b@tyonek.net

DOYON

Alatna Tribal Council
P.O. Box 70
Alatna, AK 99720
Office (907) 968–2304
Fax (907) 968–2305

Allakaket Tribal Council
P.O. Box 50
Allakaket, AK 99720
Office (907) 968–2237
Fax (907) 968–2233
Email sandra_aug27@hotmail.com

Anvik Tribal Council
P.O. Box 10
Anvik, AK 99558
Office (907) 663–6322
Fax (907) 663–6357
Email anviktribal@anviktribal.net

Arctic Village Traditional Council
P.O. Box 22069
Arctic Village, AK 99722
Office (907) 587–5990
Fax (907) 587–5128
Email av_council@hotmail.com

Beaver Village Council
P.O. Box 24029
Beaver, AK 99724
Office (907) 628–6126
Fax (907) 628–6815
Email beavercouncil@hotmail.com

Birch Creek Tribal Council
P.O. Box KBC
Fort Yukon, AK 99740
Office (907) 221–2211
Fax (907) 221–2312
Email gene_payne@hotmail.com

Canyon Village Traditional Council
P.O. Box 13
Fort Yukon, AK 99740
Office (907) 662–2502

Chalkyitsik Village Council
P.O. Box 57
Chalkyitsik, AK 99788
Office (907) 848–8117/8119
Fax (907) 848–8986
Email pardue_777@hotmail.com

Circle Native Village Council
P.O. Box 89
Circle, AK 99733
Office (907) 773–2822
Fax (907) 773–2823

Dot Lake Village Council
P.O. Box 2279
Dot Lake, AK 99737
Office (907) 882–2695
Fax (907) 882–5558
Email dotlake@aitc.org

Eagle Traditional Council
P.O. Box 19
Eagle, AK 99738
Office (907) 547–2281
Fax (907) 547–2318

Evansville Tribal Council
P.O. Box 26087
Bettles, AK 99726
Office (907) 692–5005
Fax (907) 692–5006
Email naomicoStello@starband.net

(Ft Yukon) Gwich'in Tribal Government
P.O. Box 126
Fort Yukon, AK 99740
Office (907) 662–2581
Fax (907) 662–2222
Email mary_beth_solomon@hotmail.com

(Galena) Louden Tribal Council
P.O. Box 244
Galena, AK 99741
Office (907) 656–1711
Fax (907) 656–1716
Email theresaburley@hotmail.com;
march_runner@yahoo.com

Grayling IRA Council
P.O. Box 49
Grayling, AK 99590
Office (907) 453–5116
Fax (907) 453–5146
Email sue.gochenauer@tananachiefs.org

Healy Lake Traditional Council
P.O. Box 73158
Fairbanks, AK 99707–3158
Office (907) 479–0638
Fax (907) 479–0639
Email jlpolston1@hotmail.com

Holy Cross Tribal Council
P.O. Box 89
Holy Cross, AK 99602
Office (907) 476–7124
Fax (907) 476–7132
Email holycrosstribe@hotmail.com

Hughes Village Council
P.O. Box 45029
Hughes, AK 99745
Office (907) 889–2239
Fax (907) 889–2252
Email janet.bifelt@tananachiefs.org

Huslia Village Council
P.O. Box 70
Huslia, AK 99746
Office (907) 829–2410
Fax (907) 829–2409
Email huslia.tribal.council@hotmail.com

Kaltag Tribal Council
P.O. Box 129
Kaltag, AK 99748
Office (907) 534–2224
Fax (907) 534–2299
Email ktc_tribe@hotmail.com

Koyukuk Tribal Council
P.O. Box 109
Koyukuk, AK 99754
Office (907) 927–2253
Fax (907) 927–2220
Email cynthia.pilot@tananachiefs.org

Lake Minchumina Traditional Council
P.O. Box 53
Kaktovik, AK 99747
Office (907) 455–9555

Manley Traditional Council
P.O. Box 105
Manley Hot Springs, AK 99756
Office (907) 672–3177
Fax (907) 672–3200
Email jw69p11@hotmail.com
elizabeth.woods@tananachiefs.org

McGrath Native Village Council
P.O. Box 134
McGrath, AK 99627
Office (907) 524–3024
Fax (907) 524–3899
Email mnvc@mcgrathalaska.net

Minto Village Council
P.O. Box 26
Minto, AK 99758
Office (907) 798–7112
Fax (907) 798–7627
Email mintovillagecouncil@hotmail.com

Nenana Native Council
P.O. Box 369
Nenana, AK 99760
Office (907) 832–5461
Fax (907) 832–1077
Email nibor652004@yahoo.com

Nikolai Edzeno' Village Council
P.O. Box 9105
Nikolai, AK 99691
Office (907) 293–2311
Fax (907) 293–2481
Email agnes.tony@tananachiefs.org

Northway Village
P.O. Box 516
Northway, AK 99764
Office (907) 778–2311
Fax (907) 778–2220
Email dnnvc@yahoo.com

Nulato Tribal Council
P.O. Box 65049
Nulato, AK 99765
Office (907) 898–2339
Fax (907) 898–2207
Email nulatotribe@nulatotribe.org
www.nulatotribe.org

Rampart Village Council
P.O. Box 29
Rampart, AK 99767
Office (907) 358–3312
Fax (907) 358–3115
Email elaineeevans@hotmail.com

Ruby Tribal Council
P.O. Box 68210
Ruby, AK 99768
Office (907) 468–4479
Fax (907) 468–4474
Email rubynativecouncil@hotmail.com

Shageluk IRA Council
P.O. Box 109
Shageluk, AK 99665
Office (907) 473–8239
Fax (907) 473–8295
Email Rebecca.Wulf@tananachiefs.org

Stevens Village Council
P.O. Box 16
Stevens Village, AK 99774
Office (907) 478–7228
Fax (907) 478–7229
Email Stevensvillage@hotmail.com

Takotna Tribal Council
P.O. Box 7529
Takotna, AK 99675
Office (907) 298–2212
Fax (907) 298–2314
Email takotnatc@yahoo.com

Tanacross Village Council
P.O. Box 76009
Tanacross, AK 99776
Office (907) 883–5024
Fax (907) 883–4497
Email e.sanford@nativevillageof
tanacross.com
www.nativevillageoftanacross.com

Native Village of Tanana
P.O. Box 130
Tanana, AK 99777
Office (907) 366–7170
Fax (907) 366–7195
Email tananatribalcouncil@hotmail.com

Telida Village
3060 N Lazy 8 Court, Suite 2 PM424
Wasilla, AK 99654

Tetlin Tribal Council
P.O. Box TTL
Tetlin, AK 99779
Office (907) 324–2130
Fax (907) 324–2131

Venetie Village Council
P.O. Box 81119
Venetie, AK 99781
Office (907) 849–8212
Fax (907) 849–8149
Email ninafrank@hotmail.com

KONIAG

Native Village of Afognak
204 E. Rezanof Drive, Suite 100
Kodiak, AK 99615
Office (907) 486–6357
Fax (907) 486–6529
Email tribe@afognak.org

Native Village of Akhiok
P.O. Box 5030
Akhiok, AK 99615
Office (907) 836–2313
Fax (907) 836–2345

** No Anton Larsen Village Council

** No Ayakulik Village Council

** No Bells Flats Village Council

Kaguyak Tribal Council
P.O. Box 5078
Akhiok, AK 99615
Office (907) 836–2231
Fax (907) 836–2232

Karluk IRA Tribal Council
P.O. Box 22
Karluk, AK 99608
Office (907) 241–2218
Fax (907) 241–2208
Email A96lynn@aol.com

Larsen Bay Tribal Council
P.O. Box 50
Larsen Bay, AK 99624
Office (907) 847–2207
Fax (907) 847–2307

** No Litnik Village Council

Old Harbor Tribal Council
P.O. Box 62
Old Harbor, AK 99643
Office (907) 286–2215
Fax (907) 286–2277
Email ohtribal@hotmail.com

Ouzinkie Tribal Council
P.O. Box 130
Ouzinkie, AK 99644
Office (907) 680–2259
Fax (907) 680–2214
Email ouzclerk@starband.net

Port Lions Tribal Council
P.O. Box 69
Port Lions, AK 99550
Office (907) 454–2234
Fax (907) 454–2434
Email NVOPL@starband.net
www.portlions.net

** No Port William Village Council

Sun'aq Tribe of Kodiak
312 W. Marine Way
Kodiak, AK 99615
Office (907) 486–4449
Fax (907) 486–3361
Email stktribe@alaska.com

Uganik Village Council
General Delivery
Uganik, AK 99697

** No Uyak Village Council

Woody Island Tribal Council
P.O. Box 9009
Kodiak, AK 99615
Office (888) 414–2821
Fax (907) 486–2738
Email village@alaska.net
www.woodyisland.com

NANA

Native Village of Ambler
P.O. Box 47
Ambler, AK 99786
Office (907) 445–2196
Fax (907) 445–2181
Email ivisaappaap@ivisaappaatt.org

Native Village of Buckland
P.O. Box 67
Buckland, AK 99727
Office (907) 494–2171
Fax (907) 494–2217
Email clarencethomas@nunachiak.org

Native Village of Deering
P.O. Box 36089
Deering, AK 99736
Office (907) 363–2138
Fax (907) 363–2195
Email shelia.gregg@ipnatchiaq.org

Kiana Traditional Council
P.O. Box 69
Kiana, AK 99749–0069
Office (907) 475–2109
Fax (907) 475–2180
www.kianatraditionalcouncil.com

Native Village of Kivalina
P.O. Box 50051
Kivalina, AK 99750
Office (907) 645–2153
Fax (907) 645–2193
Email colleenekc@aol.com

Kobuk Traditional Council
P.O. Box 51039
Kobuk, AK 99751
Office (907) 948–2203
Fax (907) 948–2123
Email avb_obu@yahoo.com

Kotzebue IRA Council
P.O. Box 296
Kotzebue, AK 99752
Office (907) 442–3467
Fax (907) 442–2162
Email linda.jewel@qira.org
www.kotzebueira.org

Native Village of Noatak
P.O. Box 89
Noatak, AK 99761
Office (907) 485–2173
Fax (907) 485–2137
Email herbert.walton@nautaaq.org

Noorvik Native Community
P.O. Box 209
Noorvik, AK 99763
Office (907) 636–2144
Fax (907) 636–2284
Email hendy.ballot@nuurvik.org

Selawik Village Council
P.O. Box 59
Selawik, AK 99770
Office (907) 484–2165/2225
Fax (907) 484–2226

Native Village of Shungnak
P.O. Box 64
Shungnak, AK 99773
Office (907) 437–2163
Fax (907) 437–2183
Email crystal.ticket@issingnak.org

SEALASKA

Angoon Community Association
P.O. Box 190
Angoon, AK 99820
Office (907) 788–3411
Fax (907) 788–3412

Craig Community Association
P.O. Box 828
Craig, AK 99921
Office (907) 826–3996
Fax (907) 826–3997

Douglas Indian Association
1107 W. 8th Street, Suite #3
Juneau, AK 99801
Office (907) 364–2916
Fax (907) 364–2917

(Haines) Chilkoot Indian Association
P.O. Box 490
Haines, AK 99827
Phone 907–766–2323
Fax 907–766–2365
Email gstuckey@chilkoot-nsn.gov

Hoonah Indian Association
P.O. Box 602
Hoonah, AK 99829
Office (907) 945–3545
Fax (907) 945–3703
Email jdybdahl@hiatribe.org

Hydaburg Cooperative Association
P.O. Box 349
Hydaburg, AK 99922
Office (907) 285–3666
Fax (907) 285–3541
Email d_witwer@hotmail.com

Aukquan Traditional Council
9296 Stephan Richards Memorial Drive
Juneau, AK 99801

Organized Village of Kake
P.O. Box 316
Kake, AK 99830
Office (907) 785–6471
Fax (907) 785–4902
Email gewilliams@kakefirstnation.org

Organized Village of Kasaan
P.O. Box 26
Kasaan, AK 99950–0340
Office (907) 542–2230
Fax (907) 542–3006
Email paula@kasaan.org

Klawock Cooperative Association
P.O. Box 430
Klawock, AK 99925–0430
Office (907) 755–2265
Fax (907) 755–8800
Email tribalgirl2004@hotmail.com

Ketchikan Indian Community
2960 Tongass Avenue
Ketchikan, AK 99901
Office (907) 225–5158
Fax (907) 248–5224
www.kictribe.org

(Klukwan) Chilkat Indian Village
P.O. Box 210
Haines, AK 99827–0210
Office (907) 767–5505
Fax (907) 767–5518
Email klukwan@chilkatindianvillage.org
www.chilkatindianvillage.org

Metlakatla Indian Community
P.O. Box 8
Metlakatla, AK 99926
Office (907) 886–4441
Fax (907) 886–7997

Petersburg Indian Association
P.O. Box 1418
Petersburg, AK 99833
Office (907) 772–3636
Fax (907) 772–2990
Email tribaladmin@piatribal.org

Organized Village of Saxman
Route 2, Box 2–Saxman
Ketchikan, AK 99901
Office (907) 247–2502
Fax (907) 247–2504
Email saxmanira@kpunet.net

Sitka Tribe of Alaska
456 Katlian Street
Sitka, AK 99835
Office (907) 747–3207
Fax (907) 747–4915
Email staff@sitkatribe.gov
www.sitkatribe.org

(Skagway) Skaqua Traditional Council
P.O. Box 1157
Skagway, AK 99840
Office (907) 983–4068
Fax (907) 983–3068
Email stcadmin@skagwaytraditional.org
www.skagwaytraditional.org

Wrangell Cooperative Association
P.O. Box 868
Wrangell, AK 99929
Office (907) 874–3481
Fax (907) 874–2918
Email walkerak1@gci.net

Yakutat Tlingit Tribe
P.O. Box 418
Yakutat, AK 99689
Office (907) 784–3238
Fax (907) 784–3595
Email ysnively@ytttribe.org

RESERVATION

Metlakatla Indian Community
P.O. Box 8
Metlakatla, AK 99926
Office (907) 886–4441
Fax (907) 886–7997

FORMER RESERVES

Arctic Village Traditional Council
P.O. Box 22069
Arctic Village, AK 99722
Office (907) 587–5990
Fax (907) 587–5128
Email av_council@hotmail.com

Elim Village
P.O. Box 39010
Elim, AK 99739
Office (907) 890–3741
Fax (907) 890–3091
Email elimnativecorp@gci.net

Gambell Village
P.O. Box 101
Gambell, AK 99742
Office (907) 985–5826
Fax (907) 985–5426
Email sivuqaq@gci.net

Savoonga Village
101 West Benson Blvd. Ste 304
Anchorage, AK 99769

Tetlin Village
P.O. Box TTL
Tetlin, AK 99779

Venetie Village Council
P.O. Box 81119
Venetie, AK 99781
Office (907) 849–8212
Fax (907) 849–8149
Email ninafrank@hotmail.com

ANCSA
EDUCATION CONSORTIUM

The Ahtna Heritage Foundation
P.O. Box 213
Glennallen, AK 99588
Office (907) 822–5778
Fax (907) 822–5338
www.ahtna-inc.com/heritage_
foundation.html

The Aleut Foundation
703 W Tudor Road Suite 102
Anchorage, AK 99503
Office (907) 646–1929
Fax (907) 646–1949
Email taf@thealeutfoundation.org
www.thealeutfoundation.org/index.html

Arctic Education Foundation
P.O. Box 129
Barrow, AK 99723
Office (907) 852–8633
Fax (907) 852–2774
(800) 770–2772
Email ctdanner@asrc.com
www.arcticed.com

Bering Straits Foundation
P.O. Box 1008
Nome, AK 99762
Office (907) 443–5252
Fax (907) 443–2985
www.beringstraits.com/bsf/bsfhome.htm

Bristol Bay Native Corporation Education
Foundation
111 W. 16th Avenue, Suite 400
Anchorage, AK 99501
Office (907) 278–3602
Fax (907) 276–3925
Email pelagiol@bbnc.net
www.bbnc.net/education

Calista Scholarship Fund
301 Calista Court, Suite A
Anchorage, AK 99518–3028
Office (907) 279–5516
Fax (907) 279–8430
(800) 277–5516
www.calistacorp.com/scholarship/
default.asp

Chugach Heritage Foundation
561 E. 36th Avenue
Anchorage, AK 99503
Office (907) 550–4535
Fax (907) 550–4147
(800) 858–2768
Email ana.andersen@chugach-ak.com
www.chugachheritagefoundation.org

The CIRI Foundation
3600 San Jeronimo Drive Ste 256
Anchorage, AK 99508
Office (907) 793–3575
Fax (907) 793–3585
(800) 764–3382
www.thecirifoundation.org

Doyon Foundation
1 Doyon Place, Suite 300
Fairbanks, AK 99701
Office (907) 459–2048
Fax (907) 459–2065
(888) 478–4755 x2048
Email foundation@doyon.com
www.doyonfoundation.com

Koniag Education Foundation
6927 Old Seward Hwy. Ste 103
Anchorage, AK 99518
Office (907) 562–9093
Fax (907) 562–9023
(888) 562–9093
Email kef@alaska.com
www.koniageducation.org

Robert Aqqaluk Newlin, Sr. Memorial Trust
P.O. Box 509
Kotzebue, AK 99572
Office (907) 442–3301
Fax (907) 442–2289
(866) 442–1607
www.aqqaluktrust.com/index.html

Sealaska Heritage Institute
One Sealaska Plaza, Suite 301
Juneau, AK 99801
Office (907) 463–4844
Fax (907) 586–9293
www.sealaskaheritage.org/index.htm

The 13th Regional Heritage Foundation
1156 Industry Drive
Seattle, WA 98188–4803
Office (206) 575–6229 ext. 104
Fax (206) 575–6283
Email joann@the13thregion.com
www.the13thregion.com/heritage.html

STATEWIDE AND REGIONAL NON-PROFIT ORGANIZATIONS

STATEWIDE

Association of Alaska Housing
Authorities
4300 Boniface Parkway
Anchorage, AK 99504
Office (907) 338–3970
Fax (907) 338–4904
Email aaha@AK.net
www.AK.net/~aaha

Alaska Federation of Natives
1577 C Street, Suite 300
Anchorage, AK 99501
Office (907) 274–3611
Fax (907) 276–7989
AFNInfo@NativeFederation.org
www.nativefederation.org

Alaska Inter-Tribal Council
1569 S. Bragaw Suite 102
Anchorage, AK 99508
Office (907) 563–9334
Fax (907) 563–9337
(800) 995–9334
Email delice.calcote@aitc.org
aitc.org

Alaska Native Health Board
4000 Ambassador Dr. Ste C-ANHB
Anchorage, AK 99508
Office (907) 562–6006
Fax (907) 729–1901
www.anhb.org

Alaska Native Tribal Health Consortium
4000 Ambassador Drive
Anchorage, AK 99508
Office (907) 729–1900
Fax (907) 729–1901
Email lskonberg@anthc.org
www.anthc.org

First Alaskans Institute
606 E Street, Suite 200
Anchorage, AK 99501
Office (907) 677–1700
Fax (907) 677–1780
Email info@firstalaskans.org
www.firstalaskans.org

Native American Rights Fund
420 L Street, Suite 505
Anchorage, AK 99501
Office (907) 276–0680
Fax (907) 276–2466
www.narf.org

Rural Alaska Community Association
Program (RurAL Cap)
P.O. Box 200908
Anchorage, AK 99520
Office (907) 279–2511
Fax (907) 278–2309
(800) 478–7227
Email info@ruralcap.com
www.ruralcap.com

ANCSA Regional Corporation Presidents
& CEOs, Incorporated
P.O. Box 240766
Anchorage, AK 99524
Office (907) 339–6052
Fax (907) 339–6178

REGIONAL ORGANIZATIONS

AHTNA

Copper River Basin Regional Housing
Authority
P.O. Box 89
Glennallen, AK 99588
Office (907) 822–3633
Fax (907) 822–3662
Email jdoty@crbrha.org
www.crbrha.org

Copper River Native Association
P.O. Box H
Copper Center, AK 99573
Office (907) 822–5241
Fax (907) 822–8801
Email pbxoperator@crnative.org
www.crnative.org

ALEUT

Aleutian Housing Authority
4000 Old Seward Hwy, Ste 104
Anchorage, AK 99503
(800) 478–5614
Office (907) 563–2146
Fax (907) 563–3105
www.aleutian-housing.com

Aleutian Pribilof Islands
Association
1131 East International Airport Rd.
Anchorage, AK 99518
Office (907) 276–2700
Fax (907) 279–4351
Email apiai@apiai.org
www.apiai.com

Eastern Aleutian Tribes, Incorporated
3380 C Street, Suite 100
Anchorage AK 99503
Office (907) 277–1440
Fax (907) 277–1446
www.easternaleutiantribes.com

ARCTIC SLOPE

Arctic Slope Native Association
P.O. Box 1232
Barrow, AK 99723
Office (907) 852–2762
Fax (907) 852–2105

Inupiat Community of the Arctic Slope
P.O. Box 934
Barrow, AK 99723
Office (907) 852–4227
Fax (907) 852–4246
Email icas.recep@barrow.com

Tagiugmiullu Nunamiullu
Housing Authority
P.O. Box 409
Barrow, AK 99723
Office (907) 852–7150
Fax (907) 852–2038
Email wendy.knight@tnha.net

BERING STRAITS REGION

Bering Straits Regional Housing Authority
P.O. Box 995
Nome, AK 99762
Office (907) 443-5256
Fax (907) 443-8652
Email mahmasuk@bsrha.org

Kawerak, Incorporated
P.O. Box 948
Nome, AK 99762
Office (907) 443-5231
Fax (907) 443-4452
www.kawerak.org

Norton Sound Health Corporation
P.O. Box 966
Nome, AK 99762
Office (907) 443-3311
Fax (907) 443-3139
www.nortonsoundhealth.org

BRISTOL BAY REGION

Bristol Bay Area Health Corporation
P.O. Box 130
Dillingham, AK 99576
(800) 478-5201
Office (907) 842-5201
Fax (907) 842-9409
www.bbahc.org

Bristol Bay Housing Authority
P.O. Box 50
Dillingham, AK 99576
Office (907) 842-5956
Fax (907) 842-2784
Email bbha@bbha.org
www.bbha.org

Bristol Bay Native Association
P.O. Box 310
Dillingham, AK 99576
Office (907) 842–5257
Fax (907) 842–5932
www.bbna.com

CALISTA

Association of Village Council Presidents
(AVCP)
P.O. Box 219
Bethel, AK 99559
(800) 478–3521
Office (907) 543–7300
Fax (907) 543–3596
Email Support@avcp.org
www.avcp.org

AVCP Regional Housing Authority
P.O. Box 767
Bethel, AK 99559
Office (907) 543–3121
Fax (907) 543–4020
(800) 478–4687
Email janetmute@avcphousing.org
www.avcphousing.org

Kuskokwim Native Association
P.O. Box 127
Aniak, AK 99557
Office (907) 675–4384
Fax (907) 675–4387
www.kuskokwim.org

Yukon-Kuskokwim Health Corporation
P.O. Box 528
Bethel, AK 99559
Office (907) 543–6000
Email info@ykhc.org
www.ykhc.org

CHUGACH

Chugachmiut, Incorporated
1840 Bragaw Street Suite 110
Anchorage, AK 99508–3463
Office (907) 562–4155
Fax (907) 563–2891
Email Info@Chugachmiut.org
www.chugachmiut.org

North Pacific Rim Housing Authority
8300 King Street
Anchorage, AK 99518
Office (907) 562–1444
Fax (907) 562–1445
www.nprha-ak.org

COOK INLET

Cook Inlet Housing Authority
3510 Spenard Road
Anchorage, AK 99503
Office (907) 793–3000
Fax (907) 793–3070
Email info@cookinlethousing.org
www.cookinlethousing.org

Cook Inlet Tribal Council
3600 San Jeronimo Drive
Anchorage, AK 99508
Office (907) 793–3600
Fax (907) 793–3602
(877) 985–5900
www.citci.com

Southcentral Foundation
SCF Administration Building
4501 Diplomacy Drive
Anchorage, AK 99508
Office (907) 729–4955
Fax (907) 729–5000
(800) 478–3343
www.southcentralfoundation.com

DOYON

Interior Regional Housing Authority
828 27th Avenue
Fairbanks, AK 99701
Office (907) 452–8315
Fax (907) 456–8941
(800) 478–IRHA (4742)
Email housing@irha.org
www.irha.org

Fairbanks Native Association
605 Hughes Avenue Suite 100
Fairbanks, AK 99701–7539
Office (907) 452–1648
Fax (907) 456–4148
www.fairbanksnative.org

Tanana Chiefs Conference
122 1st Avenue Suite 600
Fairbanks, AK 99701
Office (907) 452–8251
Fax (907) 459–3850
(800) 478–6822
www.tananachiefs.org

NANA

Maniilaq Association
P.O. Box 256
Kotzebue, AK 99752
Office (907) 442–3311
Fax (907) 442–7678
(800) 478–3312
www.maniilaq.org

Northwest Inupiat Housing Authority
P.O. Box 331
Kotzebue, AK 99752–0331
Office (907) 442–3450
Fax (907) 442–3486
(888) 285–3450
Email Cnelson@nwiha.com
www.nwiha.com

SEALASKA

Baranof Island Housing Authority
P.O. Box 517
Sitka, AK 99835–0517
Office (907) 747–5088
Fax (907) 747–5701
Email bihasitka@yahoo.com

Central Council of Tlingit and Haida
Indian Tribes of Alaska
320 W. Willoughby Avenue Suite 300
Juneau, AK 99801
Office (907) 586–1432
Fax (907) 586–8970
(800) 344–1432
www.ccthita.org

Ketchikan Indian Community
2960 Tongass Avenue
Ketchikan, AK 99901
Office (907) 225–5158
Fax (907) 248–5224
www.kictribe.org

Metlakatla Housing Authority
P.O. Box 59
Metlakatla, AK 99926
Office (907) 886–6500
Fax (907) 886–6503
Email methouse@aptalaska.net

Southeast Alaska Regional Health
Consortium
3245 Hospital Drive
Juneau, AK 99801
Office (907) 463–4000
Fax (907) 463–4075
www.searhc.org

Tlingit-Haida Regional Housing Authority
P.O. Box 32237
Juneau AK 99803–2237
Office (907) 780–6868
www.thrha.org

13TH REGION

The 13th Regional Heritage Foundation
1156 Industry Drive
Seattle, WA 98188–4803
Office (206) 575–6229 x104
Fax (206) 575–6283
Email joann@the13thregion.com
www.the13thregion.com/heritage.html

ALASKA NATIVE CULTURAL CENTERS & MUSEUMS

Alaska Heritage Museum at Wells Fargo
301 W. Northern Lights Blvd., Suite 103
Anchorage, AK 99510
Office (907) 265–2834
Fax (907) 265–2860

Alaska Native Heritage Center
8800 Heritage Center Drive
Anchorage, AK 99504
(800) 315–6608
Office (907) 330–8000
Fax (907) 330–8030
Email info@alaskanative.net
www.alaskanative.net

Alaska State Museum
395 Whittier Street
Juneau, AK 99801
Office (907) 465–2901
Fax (907) 465–2976
www.museums.state.ak.us

Aleutian Pribilof Islands Association
Aleut Heritage Library & Archive
1131 E. International Airport Rd
Anchorage, AK 99518
Office (907) 276–2700
Fax (907) 279–4351
Email milliem@apiai.org
www.apiai.com

Alutiiq Museum & Archaeological
Repository
215 Mission Road Suite 101
Kodiak, AK 99615
Office (907) 486–7004
Fax (907) 486–7048
Email receptionist@alutiiqmuseum.com
www.alutiiqmuseum.com

Anchorage Museum at Rasmuson Center
121 West Seventh Avenue
Anchorage, AK 99501
Office (907) 343–6172
Fax (907) 343–6149
Email museum@AnchorageMuseum.org
www.anchoragemuseum.org

Anvik Historical Society Museum
P.O. Box 10
Anvik, AK 99558
Office (907)663–6322
Fax (907)663–6357
Email anviktribal@anviktribal.net
www.anvik.org

Arctic Studies Center, National Museum
of Natural History (Smithsonian)
121 West 7th Avenue
Anchorage, AK 99501
Office (907) 343–6162
Fax (907) 343–6130
Email crowella@si.edu
www.mnh.si.edu/arcticalaska.si.edu

Baranov Museum
Kodiak Historical Society
101 Marine Way
Kodiak, AK 99615
Phone (907) 486–5920
Email baranov@ak.net
www.baranov.us

Beringia Museum of Culture & Science
P.O. Box 948
Nome, AK 99762
Office (907) 443–4340
Fax (907) 443–4452
culture@kawerak.org
www.kawerak.org/servicedivisions/
admin/culcent.html

Carrie M. McLain Memorial Museum
P.O. Box 53
Nome, AK 99762
Office (907) 443–6630
Fax (907) 443–7955
Email museum@ci.nome.ak.us
www.nomealaska.org/museum/

Chickaloon Cultural Center
P.O. Box 1105
Chickaloon, AK 99674
Office (907) 745–0722
Fax (907) 745–7154
Email itistime@chickaloon.org
www.chickaloon.org

Chief Shakes Tribal House
P.O. Box 868
Wrangell, AK 99929
Office (907) 874–3901
Fax (907) 874–3905
Email tispeter@hotmail.com
www.wrangell.com/visitors/attractions/
history/chiefshakes/index.html

Chugach Museum and Institute
of History and Art
560 East 34th Avenue
Anchorage, AK 99503–4196
Office (907) 550–4151
Fax (907) 563–8402
ChugachMuseum@chugach-ak.com
www.chugachmuseum.org

Chugachmiut, Incorporated
1840 Bragaw Street Suite 110
Anchorage, AK 99508–3463
Office (907) 562–4155
Fax (907) 563–2891
Email Info@Chugachmiut.org
www.chugachmiut.org

Clausen Memorial Museum
203 Fram Street
Petersburg, AK 99833
Office (907) 772–3598
Fax (907) 772–2698
Email clausenmuseum@aptalaska.net
www.clausenmuseum.net

Cordova Historical Museum
P.O. Box 391
Cordova, AK 99574
Office (907) 424–6665
Fax (907) 424–6666
Email infoservices@cityofcordova.net
www.cordovamuseum.org

Eskimo Heritage Program
P.O. Box 948
Nome, AK 99762
Office (907) 443–4387
Fax (907) 443–4458
Email emenadelook@kawerak.org
www.kawerak.org/culture/index.html

Huna Heritage Foundation
9301 Glacier Highway
Juneau, AK 99801
Office (907) 523–3682
Fax (907) 789–1896
Email kmiller@hunatotem.com
www.hunaheritage.org

Ilanka Cultural Center
P.O. Box 322 — 110 Nicholoff Way
Cordova, AK 99574
Office (907) 424–7903
Fax (907) 424–3018
Email larue@nveyak.org
www.ilankacenter.org
www.nveyak.com/culturalcenter.html

Ilisagvik College
P.O. Box 749
Barrow, AK 99723
Office (907) 852–3333
Fax (907) 852–2729
(800) 478–7337
student@ilisagvik.cc
www.ilisagvik.cc

Inupiat Heritage Center
Inupiat History Language and Culture
(IHLC)
P.O. Box 69
Barrow, AK 99723
Office (907) 852–0422
Fax (907) 852–0424
www.co.north-slope.ak.us/departments/
planning/ihlchome/index.html

Isabel Miller Museum
Sitka Historical Society
330 Harbor Drive
Sitka, AK 99835
Office (907) 747–6455
Fax (907) 747–6588
Email sitkahis@ptialaska.net.
www.sitkahistory.org/museum.shtml

Juneau-Douglas City Museum
155 South Seward Street
Juneau, AK 99801
Office (907) 586–3572
Fax (907) 586–3203
Email Jane_Lindsey@ci.juneau.ak.us
www.juneau.org/parkrec/museum/

Kenai Visitors and Cultural Center
11471 Kenai Spur Highway
Kenai, AK 99611
Office (907) 283–1991
Fax (907) 283–2230
Email info@visitkenai.com
www.artskenai.com

Kenaitze Indian Tribe
P.O. Box 988
Kenai, AK 99611
Office (907) 283–3633
Fax (907) 283–3052
Email tbravo@keanitze.org
www.kenaitze.org

Ketchikan Totem Heritage Center
629 Dock Street
Ketchikan, AK 99901
Office (907) 225–5900
Fax (907) 225–5901
Email aaronb@city.ketchikan.ak.us
www.city.ketchikan.ak.us/departments/
museums/totem.html

Kootznoowoo, Incorporated
8585 Old Dairy Road, Suite 104
Juneau, AK 99801
Office (907) 790–2992
Fax (907) 790–2995
Email peter@kootznoowoo.com
www.kootznoowoo.com

Melvin Olanna Carving Center
P.O. Box 72067
Shishmaref, AK 99772
Office (907) 649–2169

Museum of the Aleutians
P.O. Box 648
Unalaska, AK 99685
Office (907) 581–5150
Fax (907) 581–6682
Email aleutians@akwisp.com
www.aleutians.org

Museums Alaska
P.O. Box 1038
Homer, AK 99603
Office (907) 235–6078
Fax (907) 235–6558
Email hawfield@alaska.net
www.museumsalaska.org

Native Village of Unalakleet
P.O. Box 270
Unalakleet, AK 99684
Office (907) 624–3622
Fax (907) 624–3621
Email unkira@kawerak.org
www.kawerak.org/tribalHomePages/
unalakleet/index.html

Nunivak Culture Center
Nuniwarmiut Piciryarata Tamaryalkuti
P.O. Box 26
Mekoryuk, AK 99630
Office (907) 827–8823
Email info@nunivak.org
www.nunivak.org

Pratt Museum
3779 Bartlett Street
Homer, AK 99603
Office (907) 235–8635
Fax (907) 235–2764
Email info@prattmuseum.org
www.prattmuseum.org

Qutekcak Native Tribe
P.O. Box 1467
Seward, AK 99664–1467
Office (907) 224–3118
Fax (907) 224–5874
Email tribaladmin@qutekcak.net
www.qutekcak.net

Sheldon Jackson Museum
104 College Drive
Sitka, AK 99835
Office (907) 747–8981
Fax (907) 747–3004
Email scott.mcadams@alaska.gov
www.museums.state.ak.us/sheldon_
jackson/sjhome.html

Sheldon Museum & Cultural Center
P.O. Box 269
Haines, AK 99827
Office (907) 766–2366
Fax (907) 766–2368
Email museumdirector@aptalaska.net
www.sheldonmuseum.org

Simon Paneak Museum
P.O. Box 21085
Anaktuvuk Pass, AK 99721
Office (907) 661–3413
Fax (907) 661–3414
www.north-slope.org/nsb/55.htm

Sitka National Historical Park
103 Monastery Street
Sitka, AK 99835
Office (907) 747–0110
Fax (907) 747–5938
Email sitk_interpretation@nts.gov
www.nps.gov/sitk/

Skagway Museum and Archive
P.O. Box 521
Skagway, AK 99840
Office (907) 983–2420
Fax (907) 983–3420
Email info@skagwaymuseum.org
www.skagwaymuseum.org

Southeast Alaska Discovery Center
50 Main Street
Ketchikan, AK 99901
Office (907) 228–6220
Fax (907) 228–6234
Email r10_ketchikan_Alaska_Info@fs.fed.us
www.fs.fed.us/r10/tongass/districts/
discoverycenter/index.html

Southeast Alaska Indian Cultural Center
106 Metlakatla Street Suite C
Sitka, AK 99835
Office (907) 747–8061
Artists (907) 747–8122
Fax (907)747–8189
Email seaicc@gci.net
uaf-db.uaf.edu/Jukebox/Sitka/program/
htm/seaicc.htm

St. Lawrence Island Ivory Co-Operative
P.O. Box 89
Gambell, AK 99742
Office (907) 985–5707 or 5823
Fax (907) 985–5927

Tanadgusix (TDX) Corporation
P.O. Box 88
St. Paul, AK 99660
Office (907) 546–2107
Fax (907) 546–2366
Email info@tanadgusix.com
www.tanadgusix.com

Tongass Historical Museum
629 Dock Street
Ketchikan, AK 99901
Office (907) 225–5600
Fax (907) 225–5602
Email michaeln@city.ketchikan.ak.us
www.city.ketchikan.ak.us/departments/
museums/tongass.html

The Seward Museum
Resurrection Bay Historical Society
P.O. Box 55
Seward, AK 99664
Office (907) 224–3902

University of Alaska Museum of the
North
P.O. Box 756960
Fairbanks, AK 99775
Office (907) 474–7505
Fax (907) 474–5469
Email museum@uaf.edu
www.uaf.edu/museum/

Valdez Museum & Historical Archive
Association, Incorporated
P.O. Box 8
Valdez, AK 99686
Office (907) 835–2764
Fax (907) 835–5800
Email info@valdezmuseum.org
www.valdezmuseum.org

Wrangell Museum
P.O. Box 1050
Wrangell, AK 99929
Office (907) 874–3770
Fax (907) 874–3785
Email museum@wrangell.com
www.wrangell.com/visitors/attractions/
history/museum/

Yupiit Piciryarait Cultural Center
P.O. Box 368
Bethel, AK 99559
Office (907) 543–4538
Fax (907) 543–4539
Email Byron_Dull@bethel.uaf.edu
www.bethel.uaf.edu/YPCC/index.html

MERGED CORPORATIONS

VILLAGE MERGERS
(*Including Former Names*)

Afognak Native Corporation
Afognak (*Natives of Afognak, Incorporated*)
Port Lions (*Port Lions Native Corporation*)

Akhiok-Kaguyak, Incorporated
Akhiok (*Natives of Akhiok, Incorporated*)
Kaguyak (*Kaguyak, Incorporated*)

Alaska Peninsula Corporation
Kokhanok (*Kokhanok Native Corporation*)
Newhalen (*Newhalen Native Corporation*)
Port Heiden (*Meshik, Incorporated*)
South Naknek (*Quinuyang, Limited*)
Ugashik (*Ugashik Native Corporation*)

Choggiung, Limited
Dillingham (*Choggiung, Limited*)
Ekuk (*Ekuk Natives, Limited*)
Portage Creek (*Ohgsenakle Corporation*)

Gana-A'Yoo, Limited
Galena (*Notaaghleedin, Limited*)
Kaltag (*Takathlee-todin, Incorporated*)
Koyukuk (*Mineelghaadza', Incorporated*)
Nulato (*Nik'aghun, Limited*)

MTNT, Limited
McGrath (*Chamai, Incorporated*)
Nikolai (*DonLee Corporation*)
Takotna (*Gold Creek, Limited*)
Telida (*Sesui, Incorporated*)

K'oyitl'ots'ina, Limited
Alatna (*Alatna Endeavors, Incorporated*)
Allakaket (*Aala Kaa K'a, Incorporated*)
Hughes (*Hadohdleekaga, Incorporated*)
Huslia (*Bin Googa, Incorporated*)

The Kuskokwim Corporation
Aniak (*Aniak, Limited*)
Chuathbaluk (*Chuathbaluk Co.*)
Crooked Creek (*Kipchaughpuk, Limited*)
Georgetown (*Georgetown, Incorporated*)
Lower Kalskag (*Lower Kalskag, Incorporated*)
Napaimute (*Napaimute, Incorporated*)
Red Devil (*Red Devil, Incorporated*)
Sleetmute (*Sleetmute, Limited*)
Stony River (*Stony River, Limited*)
Upper Kalskag (*Upper Kalskag, Incorporated*)

VILLAGE/REGION MERGERS

Ahtna, Incorporated
Cantwell (*Cantwell Yedetena Na Corporation*)
Chistochina (*Cheesh-na, Incorporated*)
Copper Center (*Kluti-kaah Corporation*)
Gakona (*Gakona Corporation*)
Gulkana (*Sta-keh Corporation*)
Mentasta Lake (*Mentasta, Incorporated*)
Tazlina (*Tazlina, Incorporated*)

Koniag, Incorporated
Karluk (*Karluk Native Corporation*)

NANA, Incorporated
Ambler (*Ivisaapaagmiit Corporation*)
Buckland (*Nunachiak Corporation*)
Deering (*Deering Ipnatchiak Corporation*)
Kiana (*Katyaak Corporation*)
Kivalina (*Kivalina Sinuakmeut Corporation*)
Kobuk (*Koovukmeut, Incorporated*)
Noatak (*Noatak Napaaktukmeut Corporation*)
Noorvik (*Putoo Corporation*)
Selawik (*Akuliuk, Incorporated*)
Shungnak (*Isingnakmeut, Incorporated*)

WORKS CITED

1. Alaska Natives Commission. 1994. Final Report, Volume 1. Anchorage: Joint Federal-State Commission on Policies and Program Affecting Alaska Natives.

2. Arnold, Robert. 1978. Alaska Native Land Claims. Anchorage: The Alaska Native Foundation.

3. Berry, Mary Clay. 1975. The Alaska Pipeline, The Politics of Oil and Native Land Claims. Bloomington & London: Indiana University Press.

4. Dauenhauer, Nora Marks, Richard Dauenhauer. 1994. Haa Kusteeyi, Our Culture: Tlingit Life Stories. Juneau, Seattle and London: University of Washington Press, Sealaska Heritage Foundation.

5. Federal Field Committee for Development Planning in Alaska. 1968. Alaska Natives and the Land. Anchorage, Washington, D.C.: U.S. Government Printing Office.

6. Fortuine, Robert. 1986. Chills and Fever: Health and Disease in the Early History of Alaska. Anchorage: University of Alaska Press.

7. Gray, Nick. 1966. "Nick Gray's Speech." State Wide Native Conference, October 19, 1966.

8. Groh, Clifford John. 1976. "Oil, Money, Land and Power: The Passage of the Alaska Native Claims Settlement Act of 1971." diss., Harvard Kennedy School of Politics.

9. Hensley, William L. "What Rights to Land Have the Alaskan Natives?" University of Alaska Constitutional Law, 17 May 1966.

10. Huhndorf, Roy M. 1991. Reflections on the Alaska Native Experience. Edited by A.J. McClanahan. Anchorage: The CIRI Foundation.

11. McClanahan, A.J. "In 1966: It Took Money, an Organization and a Paper," CIRI Shareholder Update, Vol. 23, No. 9, November/December 1998, 4/7.

12. McClanahan, A.J., Julee Duhrsen. 2002. "Native Corporations: An Epic Story Benefiting Alaska," ANCSA Regional Corporation Presidents/ CEOs, 1–16.

13. McClanahan, A.J. 1986. Our Stories, Our Lives. Anchorage: The CIRI Foundation.

14. Morgan, Lael. 1988. Art and Eskimo Power The Life and Times of Alaskan Howard Rock. Fairbanks: Epicenter Press.

15. Naske, Claus-M., Herman E. Slotnick. 1979, Alaska, A History of the 49th State. Grand Rapids: William B. Eerdmans Publishing Co.

16. Peratrovich, betsy. Personal papers.

17. Public Law 92–203. 1971. 92nd Congress.

18. Stein, Gary C. 1976. "Uprooted Native Casualties of the Aleutian Campaign of World War II." Fairbanks: University of Alaska Fairbanks.

19. The ANCSA Regional Corporation Presidents and CEOs.2007. Alaska Native Corporations 2005 Economic Data. Anchorage, Walsh Sheppard.

20. Trailblazer. 1965. "Personality of the Month, Nick Gray," Cook Inlet Native Association.

21. U.S. House Committee on Interior and Insular Affairs. Hearings before the Subcommittee on Indian Affairs, H.R.

13142 and H.R. 10193, 91st Congress, 1st sess., 4,5,6 August 1969 and 9 September 1969.

22. U.S. House Committee on Interior and Insular Affairs. Hearings before the Subcommittee on Indian Affairs, H.R. 13142, H.R. 10193 and H.R. 14212, 91st Congress, 1st sess., 17, 18 October 1969.

23. U.S. Senate. 1971. Alaska Native Claims Settlement Act of 1971, Report together withAdditional and Supplemental Views.

24. U.S. Senate Committee on Interior and Insular Affairs (1968). Hearings on Alaska Native Land Claims, S. 1964, S. 2690, S. 2020 and S. 3586, 90th Congress, 2nd sess., 12 July 1968.

25. U.S. Senate Committee on Interior and Insular Affairs (1968). Hearings on Alaska Native Land Claims, S. 2906, S. 1964, S. 2690, S. 2020, 90th Congress, 2nd sess., 8–10 February 1968.

26. U.S. Senate Committee on Interior and Insular Affairs (1969). Hearings on Alaska Native Land Claims, S. 1830, 91st Congress, 1st sess., 7–8 August 1969, 534.

27. U.S. Senate Committee on Interior and Insular Affairs (1971). Hearings on Alaska Native Land Claims, S. 35, S. 835, and S. 1571, 92nd Congress, 1st sess., 29 August 1971.

28. Van Ness, Feldman, Sutcliffe, Curtis & Levenberg. 1981. RE: Issues Confronting the Alaska Native People-Memorandum. Washington, D.C.: A Professional Corporation.

29. Wolfe, Robert J. 1982. "Alaska's Great Sickness, 1900: Measles and Influenza in a Virgin Soil Population."

Proceedings of the American Philosophical Society.

INTERVIEWS BY AUTHOR

1. Angasan, Trefon, tape recording, 28 July 1998.

2. Boyko, Edgar Paul, tape recording, 7 May 1999.

3. Chase, Sophie, tape recording, 5 April 1999.

4. Irvin, George, telephone interview, winter 2001.

5. Kroloff, Mark, interview, winter 2001.

6. Mallott, Byron, tape recording, 23 July 1998 and 30 November 1998, CIRI, Anchorage; 36. telephone interview, winter 2002.

7. Martin, Stella, tape recording, 22 April 1999.

8. Shively, John, tape recording, 17 December 1998.

WEBSITE REFERENCES

Department of Commerce, Community and Economic Development
Alaska Community Database, Community Information Summaries (CIS)
www.commerce.state.ak.us/dca/commdb/CF_CIS.htm

National Congress of American Indians
Alaska Tribes
www.ncai.org/index.php?id=126&selectpro_area=3

Inuit Circumpolar Conference Alaska Communities
www.iccalaska.org/taxonomy_menu/3

Alaska Bureau of Indian Affairs
www.doi.gov/bureau-indian-affairs.html

Tanana Chiefs Conference
Tribes & Villages
www.tananachiefs.org/tribes/index.shtml

COMMUNITY REFERENCE GUIDE

Chefornak
  Chefarnrmute Incorporated 65
  Chefornak Traditional Council 82
Chenega Bay
  Chenega IRA 85
Chevak
  Chevak Company Corporation 65
  Chevak Traditional Council 82
Chickaloon
  Chickaloon Cultural Center 100
  Chickaloon Moose Creek Native
  Association, Incorporated 69
  Chickaloon Village Traditional Council 86
Chignik
  Chignik Bay Tribal Council 79
  Uyak, Incorporated 73
Chignik Lagoon
  Chignik Lagoon Native Corporation 62
  Native Village of Chignik Lagoon 79
Chignik Lake
  Chignik Lake Traditional Council 79
  Chignik River Limited 62
Chistochina
  Chistochina Tribal Council 75
Chitina
  Chitina Native Corporation 59
  Chitina Village Council 75
Chuathbaluk
  (Chuathbaluk)The Kuskokwim
  Corporation 65
  Chuathbaluk Traditional Council 82
Chuloonawick
  Chuloonawick Corporation 65
  Native Village of Chuloonawick 82
Circle
  (Circle) Danzhit Hanlaii Corporation 70
  Circle Native Village Council 87
Clark's Point
  Clark's Point Village Council 79
  Saguyak, Incorporated 62
Copper Center
  Copper River Native Association 97
  Native Village of Kluti-Kaah (Copper
  Center) 75
Council
  Council Native Corporation 61
  Council Traditional Council 77
Craig
  Craig Community Association 91
  (Craig) Shaan-Seet, Incorporated 73

Crooked Creek
  (Crooked Creek) The Kuskokwim
  Corporation 65
  Crooked Creek Traditional Council 82

D

Deering
  Native Village of Deering 90
Dillingham
  Aleknagik Natives Limited 62
  Bristol Bay Area Health Corporation 97
  Bristol Bay Housing Authority 97
  Bristol Bay Native Association 98
  (Dillingham) Choggiung, Limited 62
  (Dillingham) Curyung Tribal Council 79
  Ekuk Village Council 79
  Ekwok Natives Limited 62
Diomede
  (Diomede) Inalik Native Corporation 61
  Native Village of Diomede IRA
  Council 77
Dot Lake
  Dot Lake Native Corporation 70
  Dot Lake Village Council 87
Douglas
  Douglas Indian Association 91
  Juneau-Douglas City Museum 101

E

Eagle
  Eagle Traditional Council 87
  Hungwitchin Corporation 70
Eek
  Eek Traditional Council 82
  Iqfijouaq Company, Incorporated 65
Egegik
  Becharof Corporation 62
  Egegik Village Tribal Council 79
Eklutna
  Eklutna, Incorporated 69
  Native Village of Eklutna 86
Ekuk
  (Ekuk) Choggiung, Limited 62
  Ekuk Village Council 79
Ekwok
  Ekwok Natives Limited 62
  Ekwok Village Council 79
Elim
  Elim Native Corporation 61
  Native Village of Elim 77
  Elim Village 93

Metlakatla
Metlakatla Housing Authority 99
Metlakatla Indian Community 92, 93
Minto
Minto Village Council 88
Seth-De-Ya-Ah Corporation 71
Mountain Village
Asa'Carsarmiut Tribal Council 83
Azachorok Incorporated 66

N

Naknek
Naknek Village Council 80
Paug-Vik Incorporated, Limited 63
Nanwalek
English Bay General Store 68
Nanwalek IRA Council 86
Napaimute
(Napaimute) The Kuskokwim
Corporation 67
Native Village of Napaimute 84
Napakiak
Napakiak Corporation 67
Napakiak IRA Council 84
Napaskiak
Napaskiak, Incorporated 67
Native Village of Napaskiak 84
Oscarville Native Corporation 67
Oscarville Traditional Council 84
Nelson Lagoon
Native Village of Nelson Lagoon 76
Nelson Lagoon Corporation 59
Nenana
Nenana Native Council 88
Toghotthele Corporation 71
Newhalen
(Newhalen) Alaska Peninsula
Corporation 63
Newhalen Tribal Council 80
New Stuyahok
New Stuyahok Traditional Council 80
Stuyahok Limited 63
Newtok
Newtok Corporation 67
Newtok Traditional Council 84
Nightmute
Chinuruk, Incorporated 67
Nightmute Traditional Council 84
Umkumiut Tribal Council 85

Nikolai
Nikolai Edzeno' Village Council 88
(Nikolai) MTNT Limited 71
Nikolski
Chaluka Corporation 59
Native Village of Nikolski 76
Ninilchik
Ninilchik Native Association,
Incorporated 69
Ninilchik Traditional Council 86
Noatak
Native Village of Noatak 91
Nome
Beringia Museum of Culture &
Science 100
Bering Straits Foundation 94
Bering Straits Native Corporation 39
Bering Straits Regional Housing
Authority 97
Carrie M. McLain Memorial Museum 100
Council Native Corporation 61
Council Traditional Council 77
Eskimo Heritage Program 101
Kawerak, Incorporated 97
King Island Native Community 77
King Island Native Corporation 61
Nome Eskimo Community 78
Norton Sound Health Corporation 97
Sitnasuak Native Corporation 61
Solomon Native Corporation 61
Solomon Traditional Council 78
Nondalton
Kijik Corporation 63
Nondalton Tribal Council 80
Noorvik
Noorvik Native Community 91
Northway
Northway Natives, Incorporated 71
Northway Village 88
Nuiqsut
Kuukpik Corporation 60
Native Village of Nuiqsut 77
Nulato
(Nulato) Gana-A' Yoo Limited 71
Nulato Tribal Council 89
Nunam Iqua
Native Village of Nunam Iqua 85
Swan Lake Corporation 68
Nunapitchuk
Native Village of Nunapitchuk 84
Nunapitchuk, Limited 67

INDEX

A

O

P

Q

R

S